A Present For An Apprentice, Or, A Sure Guide To Esteem And Wealth: With Rules For His Conduct To His Master And In The World

Sir John Barnard

A

PRESENT

FOR

AN APPRENTICE

OR, A

SURE GUIDE

TO

ESTEEM AND WEAL

WITH RULES FOR HIS CONDUCT TO B

AND IN THE WORLD.

BY A LATE

LORD MAYOR OF LOND

THIRD EDITION,

Corrected and enlarged, from a Copy found
thor's Papers since the publication of the

By JOHN JOSE PH STOCKDA
Editor of the School Key, GEORGIA, and Tra
VOLTAIRE'S CHARLES XII. &c.

LONDON:
PRINTED FOR JOHN JOSEPH STOCKDA
No. 41, PALL MALL.

1807.
Price 3s.

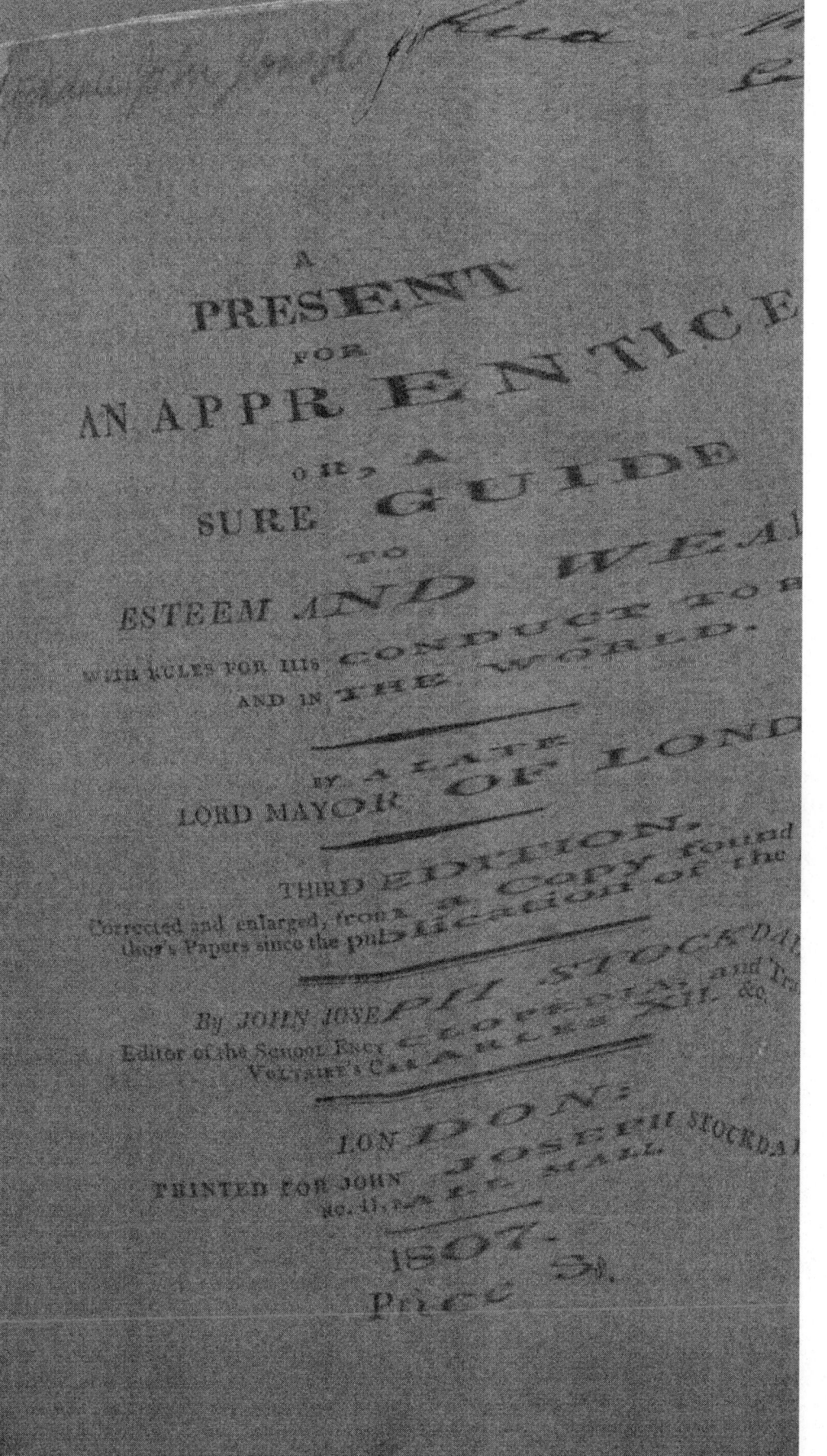

A
PRESENT
FOR
AN APPRENTICE:
OR, A
SURE GUIDE
TO
ESTEEM AND WEALTH

WITH RULES FOR HIS CONDUCT TO HIS MASTER,

AND IN THE WORLD.

BY A LATE

LORD MAYOR OF LONDON,

THIRD EDITION,

Corrected and enlarged, from a Copy found among the Au-
thor's Papers since the publication of the former, &c.

By *JOHN JOSEPH STOCKDALE,*

Editor of the SCHOOL ENCYCLOPEDIA, and Translator of
VOLTAIRE'S CHARLES XII. &c.

LONDON:

PRINTED FOR JOHN JOSEPH STOCKDALE,
NO. 41, PALL MALL.

1807.

Price 3s.

1860, Jan. 2.
By Exchange of
Duplicates.

T. Gillet, Printer, Wild-Court.

TO

SIR J. W. ANDERSON, BART.

MEMBER OF PARLIAMENT, ALDERMAN, AND LATE
LORD MAYOR OF THE CITY OF LONDON,
&c. &c. &c.

———

SIR,

THE rules, both moral and economic, laid down in the following tract are so manifestly founded on right reason, and conducive to a virtuous and happy life, that they need neither patronage, nor recommendation.

But precepts resemble pictures; they have form and colour, but want life and motion; and, to render them truly effi-cacious, they ought to be enforced by ob-vious and unquestionable examples.

If, therefore, our august metropolis is honoured with a living character, in which all the virtues, that are here inculcated as worthy the ambition of youth, appear in their strongest and most amiable light; and in which all the duties of public and private life, the citizen and patriot are minutely understood, and greatly discharged, it would be an absurdity to publish an essay of this nature, without prefixing the name, to which these noble talents belong, in the front of it. *Be what you see,* carrying with it a much more commanding force, than *be what you read!* and Virtue herself becoming more venerable, when countenanced by such an illustrious authority.

It is possible Sir, you may be offended with the application of what is here advanced: but I cannot be apprehensive of one man's resentment, when I am doing a sensible pleasure to all the world beside.

I am, with true respect, Sir,

Your most obedient,

and most humble servant,

THE EDITOR.

ADVERTISEMENT.

THE Dedication which I have taken the liberty to address unaltered, except in its superscription, was, in the former editions of the work here republished, addressed to Sir JOHN BARNARD. Although I have not the honor either to know, or to be personally acquainted with the present subject of it, conceiving that a book of this nature might derive some advantage from being placed under the protection of a City Magistrate, whose conduct, public and private, has obtained him the confi-

ADVERTISEMENT.

dence and esteem of his fellow-citi-
zens, I shall make no apology for
my choice of the personage whom
I have, with that view, selected.

J. J. STOCKDALE.

CONTENTS.

Lying - - - -	page 13
Dishonesty - - - -	15
Connivance - - - -	17
Fidelity - - - -	ib.
Temperance - - - -	18
Pleasure - - - -	19
Excess in eating - - -	21
——— drinking - - -	22
——— dress - - -	24
Government of the tongue - -	26
Talking of one's-self - -	27
Ill-natured jests - - -	28
Offending women - - -	29
Family secrets - - -	31
Secrets reposed - - -	32
One's own secrets - - -	33
Expectations - - -	34
Other people's quarrels - -	35
Tale bearing - - -	36
One's own quarrels - -	37
Affability - - - -	39
Frugality - - - -	40
Credit - - - -	41
Thrift - - - -	42
Master's cash - - -	43
Industry - - - -	44
Value of time - - -	50
Company - - - -	51
Men of sense - - -	60
The vulgar - - -	61
Sots - - - -	62
False complaisance - -	63
Friendship - - -	ib.
Choice of friends - -	66
Bonds and securities - -	67
Female servants - -	70
Fellow 'prentices - -	72
Recreations - - -	73
Cheap pleasures - -	75
Fencing and dancing - -	76
Music - - - -	78
Play house - - -	80
Gaming - - - -	81

CONTENTS.

Company of the ladies	page 84
Inconstancy	89
Masquerades	90
Horse-keeping	91
Persons proper to deal with	94
Fair professions	96
Suspicions	97
Rash resentments	98
Complacency	100
Tempers and faces of men to be studied	101
Artificial insensibility	107
Dissimulation of injuries	108
Irresolution and indolence	110
Choice of opportunities	111
Behaviour to the choleric	112
Safest to deal with those on one's own level	113
Important affairs to be managed in person	115
Rumours and tales	117
Letters	118
Caution in setting up	119
To serve first as journeyman	121
Great rents	123
Fine shops	125
Servants	127
——— familiarity with	130
——— trusting with secrets	131
——— not to be oppressed	133
——— to be used with lenity	135
Taking apprentices	137
Choice of a wife	138
Beauty	143
Good-nature	144
A good manager	146
Religious disposition	148
Portion	149
Poor relations	152
Courtship	153
Wedding day	156
Complaisance after marriage	ib.
Education of children	163
Politics	164
Religion	167

A PRESENT

FOR

AN APPRENTICE,

&c.

DEAR SON,

HAVING already done all that is
necessary in the article of expence,
for your entering gracefully on the
stage of the world, I have considered
what might yet be added to your acting your part well, in order to come
off with applause.

Recollecting, therefore, that life
is a scene of care, and prudence, generally, the child of experience and
calamity, I have thought it advis-

B

able to make you the heir of what knowledge I am possessed of, as well as my estate ; that you may be guarded against all the snares to which youth is obnoxious and that you may be as well provided with advice in all exigencies, as when under my wing ; or as if you had already suffered all I would teach you to avoid.

It is true, that it is a task that many fathers, among whom are some names of great distinction, have undertaken already and the pieces they have obliged the world with on this subject, are yet extant : a circumstance that may seem to render this little essay of mine need-less. But these have directed their thoughts to a pitch, above the level of your station and none, that I know of, stooped so low as an apprentice; to whom, nevertheless, advice was equally necessary.

Hence you will find many articles here, not touched on by their observations ; yet such, as, when tried, will be found well-worthy your attention.   But what concerns you most is not the doctrine, but the use : for it is not so hard to give good counsel as to apply it. Young men are apt to think themselves wisest ; but that in general is impossible, because wisdom is the result of time and reflection and youth must, of course, be almost as much a stranger to the one, as the other.

You have, at least this advantage then, to trade on the stock I have already purchased ; to which if you add your own acquisitions, you may be wiser at your outset in life, than many others at the close of theirs. If therefore this precaution of mine does not answer, the error will be your own; with this terrible aggravation, that your follies will be without excuse.

I have made it my care to place you with a man of character and ability in his profession; from whom, I hope, you will receive the most cogent inducements to the exercise of virtue, by his virtuous example. Remember then, in the first place, that all duties are reciprocal and, if you hope to receive favour and indulgence from him, you must, first of all, endeavour to deserve it by your obliging and ingenuous behaviour. As you fill the character of

a servant, it will be expected you
will act as a master and, if you
acquit yourself not only inoffensive-
ly, but meritoriously, you have, as
it were, bespoken the opinion of the
world in your favour and may hope
to be encouraged, trusted and served
accordingly. The grand foundation
of which, must be an inviolable attachment to truth, both in word
and deed.

Lying.] To lye, to the prejudice
of others, argues malice and villany ;
to lye in excuse of ourselves, guilt
and cowardice ; both ways a design
to delude with false representations
of things and advantage ourselves by
the deceit. Now, however artifici-
ally we may carry on this infamous
practice for a while, in the end it is
always discovered and it is hardly to

be imagined what infinite contempt is the consequence. Nay the more plausibly we have conducted our fallacies before, the more severely shall we be censured afterwards. From that moment, we lose all trust, all credit, all society; for all men avoid a liar as a common enemy: truth itself in his mouth loses its dignity; being always suspected and often disbelieved.

If, therefore, you should ever unwarily fall into an offence, never seek to cover it over with a lye. The last fault doubles the former, and each makes the other more inexcusable; whereas what is modestly acknowledged is easily forgiven and the very confession of a small trespass, establishes an opinion that we are innocent of greater.

Dishonesty.] But truth in speech must, likewise, be accompanied by integrity in all your dealings ; for it is as impossible for a dishonest person to be a good servant, as it is for a madman or an ideot to govern himself, or others by the laws of common sense. Dare not, therefore, allow yourself even to wish to convert the property of another to your own use ; more especially, where this is committed to your charge ; for breach of trust is as heinous an aggravation of theft, as pretended friendship is of murder. If, therefore, you should be lucky in your frauds and escape without being punished or detected, you will nevertheless stand self condemned ; be ashamed to trust yourself with your own thoughts and wear in your very countenance, both the consciousness of guilt and dread of a discovery : whereas innocence looks always upwards, meets the most inquisitive and suspicious eye and stands undaunted before God and man. On the other hand, if ever your knaveries come to light, to say nothing of the penalties of the law, with what shame and confusion of face, must you appear before those you have wronged ! And with what grief of heart must your relations and friends be made eye, or ear-witnesses of your disgrace ! Nor is this all ; for, even supposing you should be convinced of your folly and sincerely abhor it for the future, you must nevertheless, be always liable to suspicion and others will have the boldness to pilfer, on the presumption that you will be understood to be the thief.

Connivance.] But it is incumbent on
you, not only to be honest yourself,
but to disdain to connive at the dishonesty of others. He that winks at
an injury that he might prevent, shares
in it ; and it is as scandalous to fear
blame or reproach for doing your
duty, as to deserve reproof for the
neglect of it ; should there be, therefore, a general confederacy, among
your fellow-servants, to abuse the
confidence or credulity of your master, divulge it the very moment you
perceive it, for fear your very silence
should suggest participation of their
guilt.

Fidelity.] There is still another
sort of fidelity which may be called
that of affection; as the other is of
action, being almost of as much consequence too and what never fails to

B 5

endear you to those in whose favour
it is employed; I mean that of de-
fending their reputations; not only
negatively, by avoiding all reproach-
ful, indecent, or even familiar terms
in speaking of them; but positively,
by endeavouring at all times, to vin-
dicate them from open aspersions,
and base insinuations of others.

Temperance.]That your integrity may
be permanent, it must be founded on
the Rock of Temperance. First, therefore banish sloth, and an inordinate
love of ease; active minds only being fit for employments and none but
the industrious either deserving, or
having a possibility to thrive. This
gave occasion to Solomon to exclaim.
" the sluggard shall be cloathed with
rags; because he cries, yet a little
more sleep, a little more slumber?"

But the folly of sleeping away one's days is obvious to the dullest capacity; it being so much time abated from our lives, and either returning us into a like condition with that we were in before our births, or anticipating that, which we may expect in the grave. In short, sleep is but a refreshment, not an employment; and, while we give way to the pleasing lethargy, we sacrifice both the duties and enjoyments of our being.

Pleasure.] Neither is it enough to avoid sloth; you must likewise fly the excesses of that enchantress, *Pleasure*. Pleasure, when it becomes our business, makes business a torment; and it is as impossible to pursue both, as to serve *God* and *Mammon.* You may perhaps, think this lesson hard to learn; but it is nevertheless, the reverse of the prophet's roll, and, if bitter in the mouth, is sweet in the belly.

To explain myself more fully on this head; do not imagine I mean by this, that, though you must live by the sweat of your brow, you most not reap the harvest of your own labours. Neither God nor man exacts it of you. I speak only of pernicious, or unlawful pleasures, such as are ranged under the word Intemperance, such as prey on the body and purse, and in the end involves the soul in their common destruction.

Excess.] Excess is a pleasurable evil, that smiles, and seduces, enchants and destroys. Fly her very first appearance then; it is not safe to be within the glance of her eye, or sound of her voice and, if you once become familiar with her, you are undone. Let me farther add, that she wears a variety of shapes all pleasing, all accommodated to flatter our appetite and inflame our desires.

To the epicure she presents delicious banquets, to the bacchanal, store of exquisite wines, to the sensualist his seraglio of mistresses, to each the allurement he is most prone to and to all a pleasing poison that not only impairs the body, but stupifies the mind, and makes us bankrupts of our lives, as well as our credit and estates.

In Eating.] Above all things then be temperate and first in *eating*. One expensive mouth will wear out six pair of hands and a shilling will appease the wants of nature more effectually, as well as more innocently, than a pound. This caution deserves your attention so much the more, as you are stationed in a city, where one of the reigning vices is the riot of a prodigal table; a riot that has been severely inveighed against by our more abstemious neighbours, and which even an effeminate *Asiatic* would blush to be reproached with.

Drinking.] However injurious this species of excess may be to the body, or the purse, it is not so criminal, in many respects, as that of living only to be a thorough-fare for wine and *strong-drink*; for he that places his supreme delight in a tavern, and is uneasy till he has drank away his senses, soon renders himself unfit for every thing else. Frolic at night is followed with pains and sickness in

the morning and then what was before the poison, is administered, as the
cure. So that a whole life is often
wasted in this expensive phrensy;
poverty itself cutting off the means,
not the inclination and a merry night
being still esteemed worth living for,
though fortune, friends and even
health itself, have deserted us; nay.
though we are never mentioned but
with contempt and disgrace, and to
warn others from the vices that have
been our undoing. When you are most
inclined to stay another bottle,
be sure to go; that is the most certain indication which can be given,
that you have drank enough. The
moment after, your reason like a
false friend, will desert you, when you
most need its assistance; you will be
ripe for every mischief, and more apt
to resent, than to follow any good

counsel which might preserve you from it.

Dress.] There is, likewise, an intemperance in *dress*, which though not so blameable or dangerous as either of the others, is nevertheless worth your care to avoid. Though this folly is not of *English* growth, it agrees so well with the soil, that it flourishes rather more here, than where it first sprung up. Pretenders at court, frequenters of public places of resort, and those who would dazzle the ladies, first adopted the fashion, and from them, though with tenfold absurdity, it has spread to the inns of court and *Royal Exchange.* Dress is, at best, but a female privilege, and, in men, argue both levity of mind, and effeminacy of manners. But, in a citizen, an affectation of this kind is never to be pardoned; in him it is a vice as well as a folly; opening a' door to extravagance, which never fails to be attended with ruin: and the prudent do not care to deal with a man who must injure either them, or himself. Wherever there is a woman in a family, there is a natural issue for all the expence that can be spared on that article and that poor wretch must have a miserable head, who would inflame his wife's follies by his own. In short, son, to lay out your money in fine clothes, may be justified in fortune-hunters, because it is their stock in trade; but in nobody else; the wall in the street or some little deference, where you are *not known*, being all the advantages attending it and, where you *are*, absurd finery is no more regarded than the poor player

on the stage, in the robes of a prince.
The fop, who came into the presence
of Henry the eighth with an hundred
tenements upon his back, would
have had twice as many hats off, if
he had annually put the rents into
his pocket. It is, therefore, wisdom
to wear such apparel as suits your
condition; not sordid and beggarly,
nor foppish and conceited; agreeably
to what the poet puts in the father's
mouth, speaking to his son of his habit, which he advises to be " rich,
not gaudy, nor expressed in fancy."

Government of the tongue.] *The art,
or virtue of holding your tongue* is the
next thing I shall lay before you;
both a rare and an excellent quality
and what contributes greatly to our
ease and prosperity. In general, therefore, remember it is as dangerous to.

fall in love with one's own voice, as one's own face. Those that talk much, cannot always talk well, and may much oftener incur censure than praise. Few people care to be eclipsed and a superiority of sense is as ill brooked, as a superiority of beauty, or fortune. If you are wise, therefore, talk little, but hear much. What you are to learn from yourself must be by thinking and from others by speech. Let them find tongue then, and you ear; by which means, such as are pleased with themselves, which are the gross of mankind, will, likewise be pleased with you and you will be doubly paid for your attention, both in affection and knowledge.

Talking of one's self.] When people *talk of themselves* lend both your ears ;

it is the surest way to learn mankind; for let men be ever so much upon their guard, it is odds if some such escape is not made, as is a sufficient clew to the whole character. I need not observe to you that, for the very same reason, you are never to make yourself the subject of your own conversation; though I hope you will have no vices to conceal, all men have infirmities and, next to the rooting them out, which is perhaps impossible, is the concealing them.

Ill-natured jests.] If it is dangerous to speak of ourselves, it is much more so to take *freedoms* with other people. A jest may tickle many, but if it hurts one, the resentment that follows it, may do you more injury, than the reputation, service.

Offending women.] But it is more especially dangerous to make free with the persons, or characters of *women*; for they are naturally prone to rage and, through the very frailty of their natures, seldon fail to avenge, what braver minds either overlook, or forgive. Besides, conscious of their own feebleness, they lay their designs more cunningly, and prosecute their little quarrels more implacably, than could be expected from creatures so nearly resembling angels. Fearful of disappointments, they never trust to after-games, but effect all their purposes, by one single blow; being taught, by nature, likewise, that policy of aiming at the head, not the heel and of accomplishing their vengeance after the *Italian* mode. For, however great they esteem the provocation, they seldom suffer their

anger to break out, till sure of strik-
ing home.   Hence, it is manifest
from story, that no hatred is so extreme, no revenge so close-covered,
nor so inexorable as a woman's. Wit-
ness the case of Sir *Thomas Overbury*,
whom friendship itself could not
ransom from being a victim to femi-
nine rage.   Neither does the truth,
or falsehood of what is said, alter
the case a jot ; unless by how much
the truer, by so much the more pro-
voking ; it being with them as with
Nero, "who could not bear to be
told of what he took a delight to do."
In a word, as to conceal is their principal artifice, they hate none so much
as those who endeavour to pry into
their actions.

This must not be said too com-
prehensively ; for there are many of

that sex, whose innocency suits the delicacy of their constitutions; genuine turtles, who, being free from guilt, are equally free from suspicion and malice. These deserve to be distinguished from the gloomy, desperate tribe, alluded to above, and have nothing to fear from the licencious tongues of our sex, if they can escape those of their own.

Family secrets.] Over and above these general cautions for the government of the tongue, you must, in a more particular manner, be careful of the *secrets of the family* wherein you live; from whence hardly the most indifferent circumstance must be divulged; for he, who will drop any thing indiscreetly, may very justly be thought to retain nothing and those, who are on the watch for in-

formation, will, from a very remote
hint, conjecture all the rest.

Secrets reposed in you.] I do not advise you to seek the *confidence* of
others, for, if the secret entrusted,
should happen to take air, though
you are innocent of the discovery, it
is odds but the imputation falls on
your fidelity ; but, if any such
trust is reposed in you, suffer the
torture, rather than disclose it ; besides the mischief it may occasion to
him who confided in you, it must
argue an extreme levity of mind to
leak out to one man what was com-
municated to you by another; which
last must likewise in his heart, despise you for your incontinence, and
secretly resolve never to trust his
affairs to the custody of such a sieve.

One's own secrets.] Hence I am, naturally, led to caution you, not to be *talkative* of such designs as you have in your head; of bargains to buy, or business to do. By this means, you give others an opportunity to forestall you, if they think it worth their while, and such, whose interest interferes with yours, will take the alarm and endeavour to disappoint you, to their own advantage; besides all which, it is no bad policy to take such as we mean to deal with unprepared. In brief, never talk of your designs, till they have taken place and, even then, you had better continue silent, lest it should prejudice your future dealings.

It must however be owned a very difficult task, as self is always upper-

C.

most in the mind, not to give vent,
sometimes, to the joy of having acted
with notable shrewdness and address.   That man has not half
enough of either, who cannot prevail on himself to stifle all preten-
sions to both.   To proclaim one's
skill, is to beat an alarm to those
we deal with; as he that draws
his sword puts every body else on
his guard.   And whoever is persuaded he is overmatched by you,
will never negotiate with you again;
at least, in commodities that fluc-
tuate, in their value, according to
the demand at market.

Expectations.]   Neither is it prudent to talk of our *expectations* or of
our dependencies on the promises
of others.   If we meet with disappointments instead of services, we

sink as much in our reputations, as
if they were owing to our own bad
conduct, and it is well if we are not
derided, for our credulity, into the
bargain. Some people are disin-
genuous enough to make use of all
advantages to gratify their malignity
and it must be our business to give
them as few opportunities as possible.

Other people's quarrels.] Be, likewise, warily silent in all concerns of
disputes between *others.* He that
blows the coals in quarrels he has
nothing to do with, has no right to
complain if the sparks fly in his
face; it being extremely difficult
to interfere so happily, as not to
give offence to either one party, or
the other; almost all men having
their eyes immoveably fixed on their

own interest and continuing obstinately blind to the demands of their antagonist. Therefore, you must either side with each by turns and, thereby, deceive both, or expose yourself to the disgust, and animosity of the loser, who will judge of your conduct, not according to truth, but his own selfish prejudices.

Tale bearing.] Nothing can be more scandalously odious, than officiously to carry *inflaming tales* between persons at variance and, thereby, keep up than rancour, which, for want of fresh provocations, might otherwise expire. Beside, it is as dangerous an office, as holding a wolf by the ears ; you can neither safely proceed, nor leave off and, if ever they come to an accommodation,

the incendiary is sure to be the first
sacrifice.

One's own quarrels.] In all such
cases, therefore, let your tongue be
dipped in oil, never in vinegar, and
rather endeavour to mollify, than to
irritate the wound and, even, where
you yourself may become a principal, avoid anger as much as possible,
that you may avoid giving the provocations, almost inseparable from
it. If injured, the less passion you
betray, the better you will be able
to state your case and obtain justice, and if you are the aggressor,
rudeness, reproach, disdain and contempt, but render your adversary
implacable; whereas by mildness and
good manners, the most intractable
may be qualified and the most exas-
perated, appeased.

I find I have insensibly strayed from
the government of the tongue to that
of the *heart*, and therefore it will not
be impertinent to inform you that
quarrels are easier avoided, than
made up; for which reason do not
let it be in the power of every trifle
to ruffle you. A weathercock, that
is the sport of every wind, has more
repose than a choleric man; sometimes exposed to the scorn, sometimes to the resentment, and ever to
the abhorrence of all who know him.
Rather wink at small injuries, than
be too forward to avenge them; he
that, to destroy a single bee, should
throw down the hive, instead of one
enemy, would make a thousand.

It is abundantly better to study
the good will of all, than to excite
the resentment of any; of all, I
mean, but such whose friendship is

not to be gained except by sharing in their crimes. For there is not a creature so contemptible, which may not be somewhat beneficial and whose enmity may not be as detrimental. The mouse in one fable, spared by the lion, afterwards, in gratitude, set the same lion free from the toils he was entangled in, by gnawing them to pieces and, in another, the gnat is represented challenging the lion, and having had the best of the combat.

Affability.] Make a trial, therefore, and you will always find the force of affability. Daily experience shews us, that we make only those brutes our play-fellows, which are mild and gentle, and keep those at a distance, and in chains, which we take to be our enemies.

Frugality.]   What I shall next recommend to you is *frugality*, the practice of which is expedient for all, but
especially for such as you, who are,
like the silk-worm, to spin your riches
out of your own bosom. What I shall
give you being your full share and
as much as I can afford, and what
I shall *leave* being neither decent nor
prudent for you to reckon upon ;
since, till my death, you can have
no advantage from it and it depends
on your own behaviour, whether
even then it shall be yours, or no.
I say, therefore, it is incumbent on
you to be frugal ; for, if you miscarry through the want of frugality,
your first adventure will be your
last, and I neither can, nor would
put it in your power to shipwreck
your credit again. Besides if I were
both able and willing, to retrieve

your fortune, would be a much more difficult task, than it is now to make it. You would have the same difficulties to encounter with, as you have at present and, perhaps, such prejudices into the bargain, arising from your former errors, as no endeavours might ever get the better of.

Credit.] Be, therefore, anxiously solicitous to preserve your *credit* even from suspicion; for, next to losing it, is the doubt of its being endangered. In order to do this most effectually I still say be frugal. Credit, bought at the expence of money, belongs only to persons of an estate, or such who have already made their fortunes; in every body beside, thrift approaches nearest to virtue, and will be esteemed accordingly.

C 5

Thrift.] By *thrift* I would have you to understand not only the avoiding profusion, or the limiting your expences to pounds, and shillings, but even to pence, and farthings. The neglect of trifles, as they are called, is suffering a moth to eat holes in your purse and let out all the profits of your industry. Nothing is more true than the old proverb, " that a penny saved is two-pence got." When, therefore, you wrangle for a farthing in a bargain, or refuse to throw it away in sport, do not let fools laugh you out of your economy! But leave them their jest, and keep you your money.

Remember, the most magnificent edifice was raised from one single stone and every access, how little soever, helps to raise the heap. Let a man

once begin to save, and he will soon
be convinced, that it is the strait
road to wealth. To hope it may be
gained from nothing, is to build cas-
tles in the air; but no trifle is so
small, that will not serve for a foundation. He, that hath one shilling,
may, with more ease, increase it to
five, than he procure a penny who
is not master of a farthing. It was,
on this principle that the poor dro-
ver scraped together enough to purchase a calf and, from that contemptible beginning, went gradually
on, till he became master of many
thousands a year: He that is not a
good husband in small matters, does
not deserve to be trusted with great.

Master's Cash.] But this you are
sacredly to observe; if you should
be entrusted with the custody of

your *master's cash*, look on it as a plague-sore, that, but touched, would be your utter ruin. Remember the day of account must come when the most minute trespass cannot be concealed and when scarcely an oversight will be forgiven. In cases of property men alter their very natures; are ever suspicious of wrongs and, if any are proved, incline rather to punish than to forgive. Do not be seduced then into a fault of this nature, on any consideration whatever. Though you are taught to be frugal in your own money, you are forbidden to covet another's and, while you are a servant, your master is entitled to the benefit of all your virtues.

Industry.] To be frugal is not sufficient, you must be *industrious* too.

What is saved by thrift, must be improved by diligence; for the last doubles the first, as the earth, by reflection, renders the sun-beams hot, which would, otherwise, seem but warm. What cannot be done by one stroke, is effected by many, and application and perseverance have often succeeded, even where all other means have failed; it having been often observed, that a small vessel, which makes quick and frequent returns, brings more gain to her owners, than the large hulk, which makes but few voyages, though she holds much, and is always full. " Go to the ant thou sluggard," said Solomon, " and learn thy way and be wise !" as if, in her, the power of industry was most happily and clearly illustrated. Nothing can be more ridiculous than that, because our means will not suit with our ends, we will not suit our ends to our means; or because we cannot do what we will, we will not do what we may; depriving ourselves of what is in our power, because we cannot attain things beyond it. Whereas the way to enlarge our ability, is to double our industry; for, by many repeated efforts, we may compass in the end, what, in the beginning, we despaired of.

The fool, that promises himself success without endeavours, or dispairs at the sight of difficulties, is always disappointed; on the contrary, he that is indefatigable, succeeds even beyond his expectations. Take this from me, Son: There is not a more certain sign of a *craven* spirit, than to have the edge of one's acti-

vity soon turned by opposition, as,
on the contrary, there is no disput-
ing his fortitude, who contends with
obstacles and never gives over the
pursuit, till he has reached the end
he aimed at. Indeed, to tempers of
this last kind, few things are impossible, and the historian, speaking of
Cosmo the first duke of *Tuscany*, concludes with this strong remark,
" that the Duke by patience and industry, surmounted all those difficulties, which had, otherwise, been
invincible."

To say the truth, it argues a weak
pusillanimous spirit, to sink beneath
perplexities and calamities, and rather lament one's sufferings, than attempt to remove them. If ever,
therefore, you apprehend yourself
to be, in a manner, overwhelmed

with adversities, bear up boldly against them all. It will be the longer before you sink at least, and may, perhaps, give time and opportunity for some friendly hand to interpose for your preservation. It was a sensible device that a man made use of by way of sign : a pair of compasses, with this motto : *by constancy and labour :* one foot being fixed, the other in motion. Make this a rule, and you will be very little in fortune's power. There being, humanly speaking, as certain roads to wealth, if men resolve to keep within the proper bounds, as from one city to another.

You must, moreover, make industry a part of your character as *early* as possible. Be officiously serviceable to your master on all occasions, if possible prevent his commands, understand a nod, a look, and do rather more than is required of you, than less than your duty. He merits little, that performs but just what would be exacted; but we learn to love him who takes a pleasure in his business, and seems obliged by your commands. If you should even be enjoined to do those offices which are called mean, or which you may think beneath your station, undertake them chearfully, nor betray the least disgust at the imposition. To dispute a master's will is both undutiful and unmannerly and to obey him with reluctance, or resentment, argues, you obey only through fear, whereby you have both the pain of the service and lose the merit of it too.

Value of time.]   Above all things
learn to put a due value on *time* and
husband every moment, as if it were
to be your last.   In time, is compre-
hended all we possess, enjoy, or wish
for, and in losing that, we lose them
all.   This is a lesson that can never
be too often, nor too earnestly inculcated, especially to young people;
for they are apt to flatter themselves,
they have a large stock upon their
hands and that, though days, months
and years are wantonly wasted, they
are still rich in the remainder.   But
alas! no mistake can be greater, or
more fatal.   The moments, thus
prodigally confounded, are the most
valuable that Time distils from his
limbec; they partake of the highest
flavour and breathe out the richest
odour and, as, on the one hand, they
are irretrievable, so neither, on the

other, can all the artifice of more ex-
perienced life, compensate the loss.

Company.] But I have, already,
premised that the bow of life must
not be kept continually bent. To
relax, sometimes, is, both allowable,
and even necessary ; and as, in those
hours of *recreation*, you will be most
in danger, it will behove you to be
then most vigilantly on your guard.
Companions will then be called in to
share with you in your pleasures and,
according to your choice of them,
both your character and disposition
will receive a tincture ; as water,
passing through minerals, partakes
of their taste and efficacy. This is
a tr th so universally received, that
to know a man by his company is
become proverbial ; in the natural,
as well as in the moral world. Like

associating with like and labouring continually to throw off whatever is heterogeneous. Hence we see that discordant mixtures produce nothing but broils and fermentations, till one becomes victorious ; and as what *God* has joined he will have none to put asunder, so what he has thus put asunder he forbids to be joined. I have said thus much only to convince you how impossible it will be for you to be thought a person of integrity, while you converse with the abandoned and licentious and, by herding with such, you will not only lose your character, but your virtue too; for, whatever they find you, or whatever fallacious distinctions you may make between the men and their vices, in the end the first qualify the last and you will assimulate, or grow like each other; that is to say, by becoming familiar with evil courses,

you will cease to regard them as evil
and, by ceasing to hate them you
will soon learn both to love and prac-
tise them. And this may be con-
cluded without breach of charity;
for it is extremely difficult for frail
human nature to recover its lost innocence; but as easy for it to preci-
pitate itself into all the excesses of
vanity and vice.

Nor does the danger of *bad company* affect the mind only ; say that you
preserve your integrity, which is as
bold a supposition as can be made,
by countenancing them with your
presence, and though not equally
guilty, you may be liable to equal
danger. In cases of riots and mur-
ders, all are principals and you may
be undone for another person's crime.
Nay, in cases of treason, even silence

is capital and, in such unhappy di-
lemmas, you must either betray your
friend's life, or forfeit your own.
Thus the infamous assassin, who at-
tempted the murder of one of the
Princes of *Orange*, not only brought
destruction on himself, but also on
his confident, who, though he ab-
horred the fact, yet kept the council
of the contriver and the discovery of
the last, was made merely, by observation, that he was often seen in
company with the former.

Fly, therefore the society of *sen-
sual*, or *designing* men, or expect to
forego your innocence, feel your industry, from a pleasure, become a
burden and your frugality give place
to extravagance. These mischiefs
follow in a train and when you are
linked to bad habits, it is as hard to

think of parting with them, as to plunge into a cold bath to get rid of an ague. Neither does the malignity of the contagion appear all at once; the frolic first appears harmless and, when tasted, leaves a longing relish behind it; one appointment makes way for another, one expence leads on to a second; some invite openly, some insinuate craftily and all soon grow too importunate to be denied. Some pangs of remorse you will feel on your first degeneracy and some faint resolutions you would take to be seduced no more: which will no sooner be discovered by these bawds and factors to destruction, but all arts will be used to allure you back to bear them company in the broad beaten path to ruin. Of all these, none is more to be dreaded than raillery and this

you must expect to have exercised
upon you with its full force. Business and the cares of life, will be rendered pleasantly ridiculous, looseness
and prodigality will be called living
like a gentleman and you will be up-
braided with meanness and want of
spirit, if you dare to persist in the
ways of economy and virtue. Here
then is a fair opportunity to shew
your steadiness, courage and good
sense ; encounter wit with wit, raillery with raillery and appear above
being hurt by banter ill-founded, and
jests without a sting. There is as
much true fortitude in standing such
a charge as this and being staunch to
your integrity, as facing an enemy,
in the day of battle, or rolling un-
dismayed in a tempest, when winds
and seas seem to conspire your destruction. Many men who could

stand both the last shocks, have relented in the first and, through stark impotence of mind have been undone.

I could enforce all these arguments to induce you to avoid ill company, with examples out of number; but these will every day occur to your own observation. And, as I have already pointed out to you who to avoid, I shall next direct you who to chuse, viz. persons as carefully educated and as honestly disposed as yourself. Such as have property to preserve and characters to endanger; such as are known and esteemed; whose pursuits are laudable, whose lives are temperate and whose expences' moderate. With such companions as these, you can neither contract discredit, nor degenerate into

D

excesses; you would be a mutual check to each other and your reputation would be so established that it would be the ambition of others to be admitted members of your society.

Such should be your company in general; for particulars, as a life of trade is almost incompatible with study and contemplation, and as conversation is the most natural and easy path to knowledge, select those to be your intimates, who, by being excellent in some art, science, or accomplishment, may, in the course of your acquaintance, make your very hours of amusement contribute to your improvement. For the most part, they are open and communicative and take as much pleasure in being heard, as you in being informed; whence you will attain, at your ease, what they achieved with great expence of

time and study and the knowledge,
thus procured, is easier digested and
becomes more our own, than what
we make ourselves masters of in a
more formal and contemplative way;
facts, doctrines, opinions, and arguments, being thoroughly winnowed
from their chaff, by the wind of controversy and nothing but the golden
grain remaining. Thus it is observed of *Francis* the first of *France*, that
though he came to the crown young
and unlearned, yet, by associating
with men of genius and accomplishments, he so improved himself, as to
surpass in knowledge the most learned princes of his time. I myself knew
a young gentleman, who was taken
from school to sit in the House of
Commons and had never much leisure to return to his books; yet so
well did he chuse his companions,

and make so good a use of their conversation, that nobody spoke better
on almost all points, or was better
heard ; it being immediately expected, from the characters of those he
chose to be familiar with, that he was
either already wise, or soon would be
so ; whence his youth and inexpe-
rience were so far from exposing him
to contempt, that they greatly con-
tributed to establish an universal
prejudice in his favour.

Men of sense.]   Yet further, with
men of capacity, you may not
only improve in your understand-
ing by conversing, but may have the
benefit of their whole judgment and
experience whenever any difficulty
occurs, that puzzles your own. Men
of superior sense and candour exercise a ready and flowing indulgence
wards those who intreat their fa-

vour and are never more pleased than
when they have an opportunity to
make their talents serviceable to
mankind. Prudence, address, decorum, correctness of speech, elevation
of mind and delicacy of manners are
learned in this noble school and,
without affecting the vanity of the
name, you imperceptibly become a
finished gentleman. [*The vulgar.*]
Whereas low, sordid, ignorant, vulgar spirits, would debase you to their
own level, would unlearn you all the
decencies of life and make you abhor
the good qualities you could not attain. To preside among a herd of
brutes would be no compliment to a
man and yet this ridiculous pre-emi-
nence would be all the advantage you
could expect from such boorish companions, which, likewise, if not purchased, would not be allowed; for

those who pay an equal share of the reckoning allow no precedency and our countrymen are too proud, I had like to have said too insolent, to make any concessions, unless they are paid for them.

Sots.] In advising you to shun excess of wine yourself, it must be understood I have already advised you to shun such as *are mighty to drink strong drink*. Bears and lions ought not to be more dreadful to the sober, than men made such by inflaming liquors. Danger is ever in their company and reason, on your side, is no match for the phrensy on theirs. In short, he that is drunk is possessed and though, in other cases, we *are to resist the devil, that he may fly from us,* in this, to fly from the devil, is an easier task, than to make him fly from us.

False complaisance.] I shall add but one word more on this topic. Beware of a false complaisance, or a too easy ductility in being swayed by another person's humour. If business calls, or you dislike the conversation, or you incline to go home, or whatever the call is, if it is reasonable, obey it. A man ought to be able to say no, as well as a woman. Not to have a will of one's own renders one ridiculous, even to the very persons who govern us. Take leave then resolutely, but civilly and you will find a very few instances of steadiness, on such occasions, will secure you from future importunities.

Friendship.] Though I have said much under the head of companions, it is still necessary to add something concerning friends. Friend and com-

panion are terms often used as
meaning the same thing; but no
mistake can be greater. Many
persons have variety of companions,
but how few through their whole
lives, ever meet with a friend !
Old stories, indeed, talk of friends
who mutually contended which
should die for the other, and talkative Greece has not been sparing to
trumpet out their praises. But,
even by the manner of celebrating
these heroes of friendship, it is very
evident such examples are extremely rare. Our records, at least, shew
none such. The love of interest
seems to be the reigning spirit in our
bosoms and, wherever this pure and
delicate union is to be expected,
meum and *tuum* must be words utter-
ly unknown. Friendship, therefore,
in the strict meaning of the word, is

not likely to be the growth of our
clime and, according to the idea we
entertain of it, is confined within
very narrow bounds. For example,
I may have lived, for numbers of
years, in the strictest intimacy with
a particular man; we may have ad-
ventured in the same business, shar-
ed in the same pleasures, interchang-
ed continual good offices and treated
one another with an unrestrained
confidence; but all on these premises,
that nothing should be exacted on
either side, to the prejudice of our
darling interest; that obligations
should be exactly balanced and that,
on the least rupture, we should be
free to complain mutually of mutual
ingratitude. Whence you are to
understand, that our very friendships
are but a barter of services and civilities and are not so much calculated

to gratify the honest, undesigning in-
stincts of the heart, as for snares to
re-demand our own with usury.

Choice of friends.]   This being the
foundation of modern intimacies, you
cannot be too wary in the choice of
him you would call your friend; nor
suffer your affections to be so far en-
gaged, as to be wholly at his devotion.   It is dangerous trusting one's
happiness in another person's keeping; or to be without a power to refuse, what may be your ruin to grant.
But, if ever the appearance of wisdom, integrity and every other virtue, should lead you to cultivate a
more than ordinary friendship, never
profess more than you design to make
good and, when you oblige, let it be
freely, gallantly and without the
mercenary view of a rigid equivalent.

Neither put your friend to the pain of soliciting a good office, but spare his modesty and make it appear that you are happy in an opportunity of doing him service; but in this, as in all other things, be guided by discretion. As I would never have you apply to another for what would endanger his fortune and, of course, ruin his family, so never be induced, on any consideration, to run the like risk yourself. What interest you can make, what time you can devote, what ready money you can spare for the advantage of your friend, is nobly disposed of and never upbraid him, even should he prove ungrateful.

Bonds and securities.] Bonds, notes, or securities, which it is possible, neither he, nor you, may be able to make good, I caution you, on my blessing, never to engage in. It is

not only mortgaging your whole credit and fortune, but peace of mind.
You will never think of your obligation without terror and, the nearer
the day of payment approaches, the
more exquisite will be your pangs.
In a word, I have seen as many men
dragged into ruin by these fatal in-
cumbrances, as by a life of riot and
debauchery.   Consider, therefore,
that it is a breach of friendship for
any man to ask so unreasonable a
kindness and, from that moment, be
upon your guard! it being but a
poor consolation to be pitied in calamities undeserved ; or have it said
of you, " he was a good-natured man
and nobody's enemy but his own."

In fine, as to what concerns yourself, live in such a manner, as may
challenge friendship and favour from

all men; but defend yourself with the utmost vigilance, from ever standing in need of assistance from any. Though it is a glorious thing to bestow, it is a wretched thing to apply and, over and above the tyranny, the capriciousness, ingratitude and insensibility you will expose yourself to, when reduced to such expedients, you will then see human nature in such a light, as will put you out of humour with society and make you blush that you are one of such a worthless species.

I find I have, imperceptibly, hurried too fast, and addressed you, as if you were already acting for yourself, before I have finished what is necessary for your observation, while you are under the direction of a master.

Female servants.] In that station, it will be impossible for you to avoid the company and conversation of female servants and it will be expedient, both for your ease and quiet, that you should live upon good terms with them; giving yourself no superior airs to provoke their pride, or exacting more observance from them than they are willing to pay; but it is a matter of the highest consequence for you to avoid all familiarities with them, either within doors, or without. They are, generally, persons both meanly born and bred, with very few good qualities, often with none at all, wanton, mercenary, rapacious and designing: They will make it both their study and ambition to ensnare you, affect to do you good offices, be ever ready to serve you, seem never to be so well pleased as in your company; injure the family to regale you; attempt to seduce you with smiles, blandishments and all the stratagems of intriguing hypocrisy. If you fall into the snare, the least you can expect, is to have your attention taken off your business, your time lost, your pocket drained and, perhaps, your integrity assailed to gratify their pride, or avarice, in a more prodigal manner, than you can, honestly, afford. If they happen to have a deeper reach than ordinary, they will probably aim at your utter undoing, by a clandestine marriage, in which, if wheedling, false pretences, falser caresses, and continual importunities fail, they will talk in a higher tone, take advantage of your fears and threaten you with a discovery. On all accounts, therefore, keep yourself out of the reach.

of their ambuscades, or, if you should
be so weak as to suffer yourself to be
entangled, remember nothing can
happen to you so fatal, as to be linked to a bosom-enemy for life and that
I, your friend and the world will forgive you any thing, rather than you
should shipwreck your fortune, before you are out of the harbour.

Fellow 'prentices.] Your next domestic danger will be from your fellow 'prentices; every one of which,
if less favoured, less diligent, or less
honest than yourself, will be your
enemy; not openly and above board,
but privately, maliciously and to ac-
complish your disgrace without danger to themselves. Look upon them
as spies then, but never let them
know you are on your guard. It is
honest policy, to use craft with the
crafty and the less suspicion you be-

tray, the more easy it will be to prevent their mischiefs. It is a common artifice of the guilty, to endeavour to seduce the innocent, both because the first appear more odious in the comparison with the last and because they hope the crimes of another will help to extenuate their own. Whatever then are the bad inclinations, or practices of these young profligates, they will endeavour to persuade you to become a party in them and will give themselves more pains, than their own reformation would cost them, to bring it about. But you are now sufficiently warned and you can neither expect forgiveness nor pity, if you do not preserve yourself from the danger.

Recreations.] Having now said enough upon the head of company,

I shall enlarge yet farther on that of recreations, among which reading is to be ranked the first, as not only the most innocent, but justly to be esteemed both useful and laudable. In those leisure hours, therefore, which a shop allows, though never till the business in hand is done, let books be your companions. Not such as are merely amusement, such as romance; nor deal too much with the imagination, as poetry and plays; nor distract the mind with wrangling altercations, as controversy; but history, especially that of your own country; travels, I mean such as are to be depended upon; morals, some little law, and authentic tracts on the *British constitution*. Though you are not to be so smitten with study, as to follow it to the prejudice of your business, there is no necessity for a man of business to be incapable, or unused to study. While you are young, therefore, lay in a stock of knowledge and though crude at first, it will mellow by degrees and, when the hurry of advanced life leaves you no leisure for contemplation, you will find your memory will assist you almost as well. [*Cheap pleasures.*] It is observable, that we connect the idea of expence so closely with that of diversion, that we hardly reckon those among our pleasures, which we do not pay for; but this is both bad reasoning and bad economy. The most exquisite, as well as the most innocent of all enjoyments are such as cost us least; reading, fresh air, good weather, fine landscapes and the beauties of nature. Unbend, therefore, principally with these; they afford a very quick relish while they last and leave no remorse when over.

Fencing, Dancing, &c.] Fencing and dancing are very fine accomplishments for courtiers and very good exercises for all ; but are very impertinent ingredients in the cha-character of a man of business. In the first, too little skill only exposes you to more hazard and too much is, perhaps, an inducement to seek quarrels, rather than to avoid them. The consequences of which are sometimes fatal, always dangerous. Leave then the sword in the hands of those that are to live by it and, as it would be a very ridiculous piece of foppery in you to wear one, there is no necessity for your knowing how to use it, except however the service of your country should require it. Even in the event of your considering it adviseable to enter into a corps of volunteers, I would rather have you act as a private than as an officer. The latter situation must necessarily occupy most time, and consequently subject a man in trade to most inconvenience and expence. Notwithstanding if you should wear a sword in your country's service, never in that case let it be said to be a mere ornament in your hands. Neither have the vanity, while you are in business, to appear at court. It is a privilege which you may be entitled to from your commission, but you will be more honoured in the breach, than in the observance of it.

Neither give way to the puppyism of sporting a cocked-hat at public places. A tradesman's appearance should always be clean and neat.   When a man aims at an appearance beyond what his situation entitles him to, he is generally seen to a disadvantage and almost inevitably, meets with merited contempt.

Dancing can serve only as a recommendation to women and you are always to remember you are a tradesman, not a gallant or fortune-hunter.

Music.] Music which has so much engrossed the attention of the present age, is another of those accomplishments, which is totally superfluous in such a station as yours; nay, is not only useless, but absolutely detrimental; to have one's head filled with crotchets, being a proverbial phrase to denote a man beside himself.   Frequent not, therefore, ope-

ras, and concerts, at least very rarely;
affect not any skill in compositions,
nor to determine the merit of masters, nor trust yourself to perform on
any instrument, nor keep company
with such as make music their profession. There is an infatuation at-
tends pursuits of this nature and, the
moment you attach yourself to them,
you will decline both in your credit
and fortune. Loss of time and increase of expence are the immediate
consequences. At taverns, you must
think it a favour, if a performer contributes to your entertainment, for
which you must both defray his
reckoning and load yourself and your
friends with benefit tickets, most of
which you must pay for out of your
own pocket, and what you voluntari-
ly do for one, will be demanded by
the rest; whereby you will expose

yourself to an annual rent-charge and annual solicitations.

Play-house.] For the same reason, never be prevailed upon to set your foot behind the scenes at a play-house; the creatures to be found there being but so many birds of prey that hover round, only to devour you. Full of fawning and flattery, to win your favour and, insolently ridiculing the Cit, the moment your back is turned. Content yourself, then with putting them to their proper use on the stage and entertain yourself with their humour, out of reach of their impertinence. Not that I would be understood to recommend a frequent resort to the theatres on any terms ; on the contrary, visit them but rarely and patronise them never; at any rate, till they have undergone a very thorough purgation and appear what they ought to be, the schools of refined manners and unblemished virtue.

Gaming.] But gaming is the curse that spreads the widest, and sticks the closest to the present times. All ranks and degrees of people are infected with it. It is the livelihood of many and so countenanced by all, that it is almost scandalous to forbear it, and esteemed downright illbreeding to expose it. But, wherever you are, if cards are called for, let it be a signal for you to take your leave ; nor let the proposal of a trifling stake be a bait to induce you to sit down. Adventurers heat themselves by play, as cowards do by wine and he, that began timorously, may, by degrees, surpass the whole

E

party in rasliness and extravagance.
Besides, as avarice is one of our
strongest passions, so nothing flatters
it more than play. Good success
has an irresistible charm and the reverse prompts us to put all to the
hazard, to recover our losses. Either
way nothing is more infatuating, nor
destructive.

This is but a faint sketch of the
mischiefs attending gaming, even
upon the square; but where it is
otherwise, which often happens, as
numbers have found to their cost,
what can save the wretched bubble
from imminent and inevitable ruin ?
Or who can enumerate the snares,
the blinds, the lures employed by
sharpers, to entrap their prey and
ratify the premeditated mischief? To
be safe then, keep out of the possi-

bility of danger. Strangers, however dazzling their appearance, are always to be mistrusted. Even persons, who pride themselves on their birth, rank and fortune, have, of late, been found confederates with these splendid pickpockets; and to play with your friends is an infallible receipt to lose them. For, if you plunder them, they will abandon you with resentment, and if they plunder you, they will decline an interview, that must be attended with secret ill-will, if not open reproaches. To avoid all these hazards, play not at all; but, when you find yourself giving way to the dangerous temptation, by casting your eyes on those who, live in pomp and luxury by these execrable means, let their rotten reputations and the contempt, always connected with them, deter you from

the detestable ambition of making
your way to fortune by the same in-
fernal road; or, if that reflection
proves ineffectual for your preservation, look with horror on the numbers of meagre faces that haunt gam-
ing-houses, as ghosts are said to do
the places where their treasure is bu-
ried, who earn an infamous livelihood,
by being the tools and bawds of those
very people to whom they owe their
ruin, in order to reduce others to the
like wretchedness.

Company of the ladies.] I come now
to the pleasure of conversing with
the ladies; which, as inseparable from
our constitutions and yet often pro-
ductive of very extraordinary mischiefs, is neither to be indiscreetly
indulged, nor wholly restrained. Indeed, if a more serious turn were

given to their educations, if the *Roman Cornelia* were made the model, after which they were to form themselves, I would be the first to advise you, to devote all your leisure hours to the charms of their conversation. More humanity, more address, more politeness and ingenuity would be learned in an hour by the influence of their beauty and the force of their example, than for years in the blunt and cynical dogmas of the schools. This was, undoubtedly, what the philosopher of old meant, when he advised an unpolished fellow to sacrifice to the *Graces*.

But this is beholding the sex in the most flattering light; by being early taught to admire themselves, they very seldom regard any thing else; and you may as well endeavour to set your seal upon a bubble, as to fix that mercurial spirit, which flies all off in vapour. To visit them only for your own amusement is what they never will away with and to become the instrument of theirs, is to commence slave at once, and live only to be at their devotion. From that moment, neither your friend, your will, nor your purse is your own. Nay you must alter your very character and appear not what you are, but what they would have you. Your dress, from thenceforward, cannot be too fantastical, nor your discourse too vain ; insomuch that one would conclude not only *Venus* herself to be born of froth, but all her votaries too.

Presents, pleasures, treats must always be your harbingers to bespeak your welcome ; no business is so sacred, but must be postponed in compliment to them, no expence so great, but must be incurred to please them and no friendship so dear but must be sacrificed, when they fancy it interferes with them.

When, therefore, either by accident, or choice, you venture into their insinuating company, consider them all as syrens, that have fascination in their eyes, music on their tongues and mischief in their hearts. Let your correspondence with them be only to learn their artifices, unravel their designs and caution yourself how to avoid them. Or, if your inclinations render their society necessary to your happiness, let your prudence chuse for you, not your appetite! Search out those qualities that will blend most kindly with your own and let domestic excellencies

out weigh more shining accomplishments. But of this I shall speak
more largely towards my conclusion.
At present, I shall close this topic
with observing to you that, after you
have deliberately fixed on this choice,
it is of the utmost importance to you
to make *a covenant with your eyes*, as it
is beautifully expressed in scripture,
not to wander after other objects of
desire and admiration. He that once
quits the anchor of constancy, will
be the sport of every wind and tide
of passion, for his whole life to come.
Happiness, as well as charity, ought
to begin and end at home; and, if
ever you suffer yourself to think with
disgust, or even indifference of your
wife, your days, from that unhappy
moment, will lose their relish and
your nights their tranquillity. Reproaches and debates will sadden

your meals and thwarting measures, perhaps, bring on your ruin.

Inconstancy.] Neither flatter yourself, that you will proceed but certain steps in the dangerous path of inconstancy. Once astray, it will be one of the most difficult tasks in the world to recover the right road. So many fallacious prospects will present themselves before you, so dark and intricate will appear the maze behind you, that, once in, you will be tempted to wander on and, though a variety of adventures will produce but a variety of disappointments, you will still pursue the *ignis fatuus*, till it leads you to destruction.

That I may leave no avenue to this fatal labyrinth unguarded, I advise you most earnestly to let all

E 5

your actions, intimacies, and amusements, be as unreserved, open and
avowed as posible.   The public eye,
though a very severe, is a very wholesome monitor, and many a man has
been restrained from ill courses,
merely by knowing he was observed.

Musquerades.] A masquerade, therefore, however innocent it may seem,
or however speciously it may be de-
fended, is a place you are never to be
prevailed upon, either by your own
curiosity, or the importunities of
others to visit.   It is making too
bold an experiment on human frailty
and I am convinced many persons
have ventured on crimes there, they
would otherwise have avoided, merely because they were unknown.   It
is a maxim of the poet, that " con-
" tempt of Fame begets contempt of
" Virtue;" and to this may be add-

ed, that " to be out of the reach of
" Fame is to be in the way of Vice."

Horse-keeping.] To proceed,
though riding is both an innocent
and manly exercise and I have for-
merly recommended it to you, as
most fit for you to indulge yourself
in, I have now lived long enough to
retract a great part of what I advanced on that head and see cause
to dissuade you from keeping a horse;
at least, till your circumstances, or
improved sagacity render it allowable; or your health or business necessary. And what has induced me
to alter my opinion you will find as
follows. It is, generally, observed
that the ancient, laudable parsimony
and frugality of the city is hardly
any where to be found and that luxury and expence reign in their stead;

a very great article of which is now obviously to be placed to the account of riding and the consequences that are become almost inseparable from it. The young tradesman is no sooner set up, but he searches *Smithfield* for a hunter, and having heard certain terms of jockeyship bandied about among his companions, exposes himself by using them absurdly; and is cheated ten times over, before he acquires any better skill. The charge of livery-stables is now added to those of rent, house-keeping, &c. and opportunities are panted for of producing his new equipage and sharing in the frolics of the age. Seats, palaces, public places are first visited in turn; and, as such expeditions are pre-supposed expensive, no article of prodigality is spared, nor any exorbitant bill taxed, for fear his

spirit, or his ability should be called
in question. To these succeed horse-
races and hunting matches. Intemperance in drinking is learned at the
one, an itch for gaming at the other,
and pride, folly and prodigality at
both. A country lodging is the next
step, which is not esteemed proper-
ly furnished without a mistress, who
must be kept ostentatiously, to make
her amends for moping away the
summer, out of the reach of her old
companions and the amusements of
the town. In consequence of all
this, business is cramped into one-
half of the week, that pleasure may
be indulged during the rest; and servants are entrusted with the ma-
nagement of all, who seldom fail to
put in for their share of the plunder
and, by having their master's secrets in their keeping, are less

anxious for their own. With so
many inlets for ruin, is it any wonder, to hear it takes place ; to hear
of notes discounted at a greater pre-
mium, than the most profitable trade
can pay, goods taken up in one shop
in order to be pledged at another ;
and, finally, of bills protested and
bankruptcies, with scarce effects
enough remaining to pay for taking
out the commission ? This being the
case, as fatal experience manifests it
is, do not commence jockey, till you
are sure you can sit firm on your
saddle and defy your horse to run
away with his rider.

Proper persons to deal with.] From
diversions, I now return again to
business. In the first place, deal
with those of the fairest characters
and best established circumstances ;

they can both afford to sell better
bargains and afford longer credit;
and have too much depending on
their conduct, to be easily induced
to do, or connive at a fraudulent action. Nevertheless, to be secure,
you must put yourself in no man's
power; for, if you neglect your own
interest, how can you complain of
infidelity in others; besides, though
we should allow there are numbers
of men so unfeignedly honest, that
no consideration could prevail with
them to do an immoral thing, however covered from observation: yet
experience will teach you there are
many others, who are only the coun-
terfeits of these; who make use of
virtue but as stock in trade and are
ready to bring it to market, the moment there is an opportunity to dis-

pose of it, for as much as they think
it worth.

Fair professions.] Above all, be
most cautious of those who profess
the most! especially, if their advan-
ces are sudden, extraordinary, or
without a plausible foundation. Depend upon it, all the commerce of
mankind is founded upon mutual interest and, if it is not apparent by
what means you could deserve all
these *blandishments,* conclude they
are artificial and keep yourself out
of danger. Gilding the pill is not
peculiar to apothecaries; the same
craft prevails through every scene of
life; and more mischief has been
done under the mask of friendship,
than by the most avowed and inve-
terate enmity. In such cases, men

are upon their guard and, generally speaking, very effectually provide for their own security; but where the heart is open, it is assailable and you are undone, before you suspected you were in harm's way.

Suspicion.] Although you are to beware of credulity on one hand, you are to beware of betraying your suspicions on the other. That sets fire to the train at once and of a doubtful friend, you make a certain enemy. Besides, the circumstances that justify your fears, may make but a very poor figure in evidence; and, though you may be perfectly in the right in being upon your guard, you will appear as much in the wrong in making out a charge only from your own apprehensions.

Rash resentments.] Neither is it safe, nor prudent to declare open war upon every trifling injury ; it is impossible to live without suffering and, if we give way to our resentments on all such occasions, quarrels will be, in a manner, the business of our lives. On the other hand, if ever, through accident, or human infirmity, you should be the aggressor, let it be your glory to acknowledge your fault and make instant retribution. Next to the merit of doing right, is the atoning for what is done wrong ; and, in spite of the vulgar notion, that it is mean to submit, or acknowledge a trespass, do you esteem it the height of moral gallantry. If the conquest of one's self is the most difficult of all atchievements, you will think it the noblest of all triumphs. Nor let the poverty, nor

impotence of your adversary induce
you to overlook, or despise him; for,
the weaker he is, the less courage
was required to oppose him and the
more tyranny appears in oppressing
him, merely because the odds of
strength was on your side. The
most abject of men too, may be able
to ruin the proudest; and, in the
Turkish history, you will find a story
of a prime vizier killed in the divan
by the hand of a common soldier
whom he had aggrieved. Remember, on all occasions, that anger is
an impertinent passion; if it intrudes
while you complain of, or seek redress for injuries received, truth
will be hurt by the medium through
which it is seen, and that will be esteemed prejudice, or spleen, which
is, in fact, both truth and evidence.
On the other side, if it breaks out

when you are yourself accused, it argues that a sore place is touched and your very sensibility proclaims your guilt.

Complacency.] Instead, therefore, of seeking quarrels, or husbanding debates, endeavour to make friends, if possible, of all you have concerns with.   This can be done by no means so effectually, as by an affable and courteous behaviour.   I have known a bow, a smile, or an obliging expression people a shop with customers.   In short, no rhetoric has more force than a sweet and gentle deportment; it will win favour and maintain it; will enforce what is right and excuse what is wrong.

Let this be the rule of your conduct in general; and, in particular, when induced to bestow a favour, do it, as before hinted, with a frankness that shall give it a ten fold value. Or, if applied to, for what you are obliged to refuse, let it be manifest you are governed by necessity, not choice and that you share with him, you so refuse, in the pain of the disappointment.

But there are some persons that neither affability, nor even obligations can win; those are the covetous and the proud; both of which are ungrateful soils that yield no returns. One thinking all no more than his due; and the other either laughing in his sleeve at your foolish generosity, or fancying it is only meant as a snare to render him your bubble.

Tempers of men to be studied] To

study the tempers and dispositions
of men will, therefore, be of signal
use in your commerce with the world;
to carry your own points, and secure
you from the designs of others.   In
the first of these cases, be sure never
to solicit a man against his ruling
passion; for to induce a miser to
act liberally, a coward bravely, or
a selfish man disinterestedly, ex-
ceeds all power of persuasion; and
you may as well hope to reduce all
faces to the same similitude, as work
them to such ends as contradict
their own.   Nevertheless, all may be
made serviceable, if managed with
dexterity and address.   The miser,
in particular, to secure his purse
from importunities, will give you as
much of his time, or industry as you
please.   He is willing to be on good
terms with his fellow-creatures and
will purchase their friendship on any

terms, save that of parting with his money. However sordid, therefore, his principles or practice, it is not amiss to have such a character among the number of your acquaintance; and, especially in arbitrations, nobody more deserves your confidence. He will there stickle for your interest, as if it was his own and wrangle obstinately for trifles, that you would be ashamed to mention; whence it is odds but he procures you better terms, than you either expected, or could have attained by your own endeavours.

And their faces:] To be able to turn all the different inclinations effectually to your own advantage, I would have you, however whimsical, or romantic it may at first appear, to study the expression which the hand of nature has written in every face. Men may disguise their actions, but not their inclinations and, though it is not easy to guess, by the muscles of the countenance what a man will do, it is hardly to be concealed what he wishes to have done. Judge, therefore, of characters, by what they are constitutionally and what habitually; that is to say, in other words, what they would be thought and what they really are. But principally, the last; for, however diligently a man may keep guard on his passions, they will sally out sometimes, in spite of him; and those escapes are a never-failing clue to wind the labyrinth of his life.

I say again, therefore, take your first impressions of men from their faces; and, though it is exceeding difficult to lay down rules to inform your judgment, or assist your conjectures on this occasion, you have nothing to do but to make the study familiar to you and you will very rarely be mistaken.   Observation and experience presently unveil the mystery ; and even hypocrisy can hardly preserve itself from the rigour of your scrutiny.   Not that I would advise you to be to peremptory in your decisions neither ; but compare mens faces with their actions and their actions with their faces, till, by the light mutually reflected from each other, you are able to ascertain the truth.   Nor is this custom alone serviceable in judging of a man in the gross : it will likewise help you to determine of every extempore impulse, that, for the time being, governs the heart.   Thus while you barter, purchase, solicit, or any other way confer, the uncontroulable emotions of

the countenance will more infallibly
indicate the purpose of him you
treat with, than any thing he utters
and give you earlier notice to be on
your guard. In order to do this effectually, your own eye must, warily,
watch every motion of his; especially when you are delivering what
you think will affect him most. You
must, likewise, weigh every hasty
syllable he lets fall; for these are generally the imbecilities of human
nature, as well as the involuntary
symptoms in the face; and what deliberate speeches and cool reasonings
conceal, these flash out at once,
without warning and beyond recal.
But, however curiously you examine
the eye, or heart of another, it will
be to little purpose, unless you have
art enough to conceal your own; for
you may depend upon it, if the net
appears, you will lose your game.

Artificial insensibility.] Now the best and nearest way to attain this self-continence, is to cultivate an artificial insensibility of fear, anger, sorrow and concern of any sort whatever. He that acutely feels either pain, or pleasure, cannot help expressing it some way, or other; and whoever makes the discovery, has the springs of the affections at his command and may wind them up, or let them down at pleasure; whereas he that witnesses no sensation of the mind, betrays no weakness and is wholly inaccessible. Labour then indefatigably to subdue your resentments; for, as you are to bustle through the busy world, the more exquisite your sensations are, the more frequent and more severe will be your pangs. The passions are, like the elements, excellent servants,

F 2

but dreadful masters and whoever is under their dominion, will have little leisure to do any thing, but obey their dictates.

Dissimulation of injuries.] In the particular of injuries, it is above all things necessary, sometimes, not only not to resent them, but even to dissemble the very feeling them. Whoever complains, declares he would punish if he had the power; and from that moment, your adversary both thinks his animosity justifiable and will do you all the mischief possible by way of self-defence; whereas, if you seem ignorant at the ill turn he has done you, he concludes himself safe from your expostulations, or reproaches and will believe it his interest to behave so as to avoid an explanation. Again, in wrestling with those that have more strength and power than yourself, though equity be on your side, it is ten to one but you are hurt more by contending for redress, than by the very grievance itself. Remember, then, the fable of the brazen and earthen pots and keep as far as you can from the dangerous encounter. Again, I have known many a man interpret the most innocent action or expression into an affront and, in the foolish pursuit of what he called justice, has lost the best friend he had in the world. Therefore, those forward tongues, or peevish tempers, which rather chuse to vent their present spleen, than make it give place to their future convenience, not only keep themselves in perpetual troubles, but, also, shut the door against those opportunities, which, other-

wise, might have been presented to
their advantage.

Irresolution and indolence.] Though
you must not let your actions be governed by every sudden gust of appetite, or passion that rises, you are
not, on the other hand, to deliberate
so lazily on every proposal that you
lose the occasion, while you are paus-
ing whether you shall use it. Some
fall into this aguish disease, through
doubt, irresolution and timidity;
and others through downright indolence, flattering themselves, that, if
wind and tide court them to-day,
they will do the same to-morrow.
But nothing is more dangerously fallacious; one moment sometimes offers what whole ages might be wasted in soliciting in vain. If, therefore, such a nice and delicate crisis

as this, should court your accept-
ance, be bold! be vigilant! be reso-
lute and never sleep till you have
made the most of it. There is more
reason to use economy in husbanding time, than money, since it is infinitely more valuable; and he that
does not make this the ruling maxim of his life, may be said, very per-
tinently, to shorten his days.

Choice of opportunities.] I would
further advise you, when you have
to carry any point, which depends
on the will of another, to choose the
minute of application with all the sagacity you are master of; for there
is no man living whose temper is so
even, as not to be sometimes more
liable to impression than at others.
Even contingencies govern us; we
are more inclined to generosity, when

a prosperous gale has breathed upon
us and more prone to peevishness
and obstinacy, when ruffled by perplexities, or misfortune. Some men
are even so irritated by hunger, that
till they are appeased by a hearty
dinner, they are inaccessible; and
others so reserved, and sullen, that
till a bottle or two has thawed their
frozen humours, they have neither
eyes, ears, reflection, nor understand-
ing. Such as these, therefore, are
not to be esteemed the same men
in one mood, as they arc in another;
and, if you happen to mistake the
moment, do not immediately give
out in despair, but renew the attack,
till you find the soul open and apt to
receive what direction you please to
give it.

Behaviour to the choleric.] At all

adventures, never take fire from an
angry man and oppose fury to fury;
but give the phrensy way and it will
melt into a tameness that you yourself will wonder at. From being
fiery and untractable, he will become
pliant and gentle; and, fearful that,
during his transport, he has broken
the rules of decency and decorum,
he will make a thousand concessions
to re-establish himself in your good
opinion, the least of which he would
not have borne the mention of before.
Whereas, if, on the first provocation,
you had flung away with resentment, you had not only lost your
point, but your interest in the man
for ever.

*Safest to deal with those on one's own
level.*] It is best, however, to confine
your dealings, if possible, to such as

F 5

are pretty near on your own level; where dependance may be mutual; and no great consequence to be feared from the overbearing humour of a would-be-lion, without teeth, or claws. Where such a temper happens to meet with large power, carefully avoid coming within the reach of it, such tyrants delighting to make a prey of their fellow-creatures; pleading their humour as a sufficient excuse for all manner of mischief and making use of their odds of strength to cut off every mean of reparation. In the days of Queen Mary, Philip King of Spain, her husband, demanded the guardianship of her heir, if she should have one; with certain places of strength, to confirm his authority; offering at the same time his bond, to deliver up his trust, in case the child died immediately.

But when the House, out of a false complaisance to the throne, was on the point of conceding, an unlucky question of Lord Paget; "who "should put the King's bond in "suit, in case he trespassed on the "conditions?" turned the tide at once and the proposal was rejected, I think, unanimously. Public transactions may sometimes be applied to private. Never enter into articles therefore, but where there is a reasonable prospect of recovering the penalty.

Important affairs to be managed in person.] I further recommend it to you, as another wholesome rule for your conduct, to manage all your important affairs in person if possible. More deference is generally paid to the principal, than to any delegate whatever; nor can another person be either so well instructed in your views, or so capable to improve every advantage that may arise, as yourself. If want of health, or any other equal incapacity should prevent your own attendance, rather negotiate by letter, than by the mouth of another. Your meaning may be ill understood and worse delivered. Offence may be taken at omissions, or additions of which you are wholly innocent. Your very apologies may be so misrepresented, as to inflame, instead of appease and you may be defeated in your designs, by a series of blunders, more deserving laughter, than serious and passionate expostulation. Should you ever happen to be entangled in such a ridiculous labyrinth, take it immediately upon yourself to wind your way out. A few minutes conversation will clear up the misunderstandings of a year, if there is no rancour at the bottom. For this reason, never conclude either to your friend's disadvantage, or your own, till you have had the satisfaction of canvassing the affair face to face.

Rumours and tales.] For the same reason, do not suffer yourself to be misled by idle rumours and gossiping tales. Expressions, harmless, when first let fall, receive their venom from the channel through which they are conveyed; and, by concluding at second hand, you are governed, not by the fact itself, but by the apprehensions, humours, passions, follies and even wantonnesses of other people. If then you will give these officious-tale-bearers the pleasure of listening to them, let it be with a guard upon your heart; not to suffer it to be seduced by what, perhaps, is a downright forgery, or, at least, the grossest misrepresentation. Weigh well the character of him that speaks, against his spoken of; the circumstances, views, interests of both and whatever else may help you to come at the truth, clear of prejudice, or disingenuity.

Letters.] Having advised you to treat by letters rather than message, when hindered by inconveniences from attending in person, I must take a step back to caution you to write with the utmost deliberation, seldom without taking copies and never without reading what you have written twice or thrice over. Letters are generally preserved and thence are always at hand *as a sort of evidence against you.* You cannot, therefore, write too cautiously; I will not say ambiguously, according to the maxim of Tiberius, who sometimes wrote in that manner to the senate by design, to answer his own corrupt purposes. In a word, write so, as neither to deceive others, nor expose yourself; with all the subtlety of the serpent, but the innocence of the dove.

God only knows whether I shall live to see you set up in the world; if I do not, this legacy will be almost of as much service to you, as your fortune, if you resolve to be so much your own friend, as to regard it as it deserves.

Caution in setting up.] When, there-

fore, the term of your indenture is
expired and you grow ambitious of
appearing your own master, I advise
you in the most earnest and serious
manner, to consider it as an affair
that is to influence your whole future
life. Many by their haste and pre-
cipitation in this particular, have
only hastened their own undoing;
and, to get rid of a gentle subjection,
have rendered themselves the perpetual slaves of want and wretchedness.
To set up and miscarry, is like the
blast to the blossom; if it does not
absolutely kill, it leaves it diseased
and the fruit is both worthless and
despised. Hold the rein, then, tight
on your impatience and examine the
ground over and over again, before
you start for the prize. It has been
observed that few, or none thrive,
who set up the moment they are out

of the leading-strings, as it were.
Hope has too great an ascendancy
at that time of life and the stripling
is sanguine enough to begin where
his old master left off. But, the
ship that sets out with all sail and no
ballast, is sure to turn bottom upwards; and, as I have before, more
at large, laid down, curiosity, pleasure and expence, have so strong an
influence upon the unexperienced
mind, that solicitude, and application, though the best friends a tradesman has, are dismissed without a
hearing.

To serve first as journeyman.] Would
you, therefore, be prevailed on to
tread in the same steps, that have
carried me through life with credit
to myself and prosperity to my family, serve a year or two as journey-

man to the shrewdest and most expe-
rienced person of your profession.
You will learn more dexterity and address in the procuring and dispatch of
business, during that interval, than in
the whole seven years, you had served already. It will, besides, give
you leisure to look round for a proper place to settle in, where there is
a vacancy in trade that you may
hope to fill with success ; as, likewise,
to select those dealers who are most
likely to serve you best on one hand
and to court those customers who
are the surest pay and give the largest
orders on the other. Or, if you are
too weary of servitude and dependance to endure it any longer, enter
into partnership with such a one as
is above described ; and, though you
may expect he will manage so, that
the contract shall rather incline to

his advantage, you will be a gainer upon the whole. Thenceforward, his experience, his address and his sagacity will be yours, and for the sake of his interest and character, he will be equally vigilant of yours.

Great rents.] But, if no such opportunity offers and you prepare to set out wholly on your own bottom, do not encumber yourself with a house of a greater rent, than the current profits of your business will easily pay. Many young beginners have half undone themselves, by want of foresight in this one article. Quarter days are clamorous visitants and their dues must be sliced off from the capital stock, if the product does not swell in proportion to the demand. Before, therefore, you attempt the danger-

ous experiment, make the most
exact estimate possible, of the expences you may incur and the prospects you have to make the balance
even ; and rather trade within your
compass, than beyond it.   It is
easy to enlarge your risk, but not to
contract it ; and, once out of your
depth, it is great hazard if ever you
recover your footing any more.

It is a plain, but sensible rustick
saying, " eat your brown bread
first ;" nor is there a better rule for
a young man's outset in the world.
While you continue single, you may
live within as narrow bounds as you
please ; and it is then you must begin to save, in order to be provided
for the more enlarged expence of
your future family. Besides, a plain,
frugal life is then supported most

chearfully; it is your own choice,
may be justified on the best and
most honest principles of the world,
and you have nobody's pride to
struggle with, or appetites to master
but your own. As you advance in
life and success, it will be expected
you give yourself greater indulgence;
and you may then be allowed to do
it, both reasonably and safely.

Fine shops.] Beware, likewise, of
an ostentatious beginning ; a huge,
unwieldly, tawdry front and of laying out as much to adorn a shop, as
to fill it. There is, here and there,
a street in this town, where the
shops are set out with looking-
glasses, carvings, gildings, columns
and all the ornaments of architec-
ture; where both masters and men
are beaux in their way, and make it

a science to inveigle customers by
their civilities, as well as their out-
side finery. Yet more younger sons
of good families and fortunes, from
two to ten thousand pounds, are
here wrecked, by these prodigal
stratagems, than in half the town
beside ; and all for want of proper
forethought, in estimating the certain issues, and the uncertain gains,
with proper allowance for unavoidable losses, by some customers who
cannot pay and by others who will
not. Some who are above the reach
of the law and, others beneath it.
Truly, from their wretched examples, I have often been induced to
conclude, that young sparks, who
set up with a large and affluent fortune, are not in so sure a road to
thrive, as those who are limited to a
more scanty pattern. For they first

think they may command fortune and, therefore, launch into expences without fear or wit; nor believe they can be undone, till it is too late to prevent it; whereas the last, by being ever in fear of ruin, make use of all their wit, application and industry, to be above the danger; and hence get into such a habit of temperance, solicitude and frugality, that no prosperity can get the better of; so that in process of time, every pound becomes a hundred, every hundred a thousand; and the labour of one life, enriches a whole family for ages.

Servants.] What next occurs to me is on the head of servants, who are of much more importance, both to your quiet and welfare, than you may at first imagine. By the way,

let me premise to you in general,
that they are but too frequently domestic enemies, whose views, designs
and inclinations are opposite to your
own; hating your authority, despis-
ing your person, and watching every
opportunity to injure you, even to
gratify their malice, in defect of
other more interesting motives.
Such, I say, they are in general;
and you will find all their little cun-
ning and dexterity employed to cheat
and impose upon you; for which,
in spite of our utmost caution, opportunities will not be wanting, nor
will they fail to improve them.
Some there are, however, among
them, who retain their integrity,
who consider their master's interest
as their own and who labour as indefatigably to serve it. These, indeed,
are diamonds of the first water; nor

can their endeavours be too cor-
dially accepted, or too punctually
rewarded; yet even these are not to
be trusted too much with the secret
of their own strength : importance
of any kind, being what human frailty is least able to bear. I do not
advise you to place an unlimited
confidence in any, even the most
promising; but, above all, beware
of him who fawns and flatters to insinuate himself into your favour;
for they are such, whom nature has
gifted to deceive and they study to
make the most of that dangerous
talent. In my whole life, I never
knew any of this class, who had any
thing else in view. They have generally such a consummate impudence,
that they practice their rogueries,
while they stare you in the face and

G

ever mean the most mischief, when they pretend the most service.

Familiarity with them.] Though I would have you treat your servants as your fellow-creatures, however humble their lot, I caution you to avoid all approaches to an indecent familiarity with them; for, to a proverb, it is accompanied with contempt and contempt never fails to break the neck of obedience. Those servants, that are not kept under a proper subjection, are more apt to dispute, than obey, which, if you would preserve your authority, you are not to permit even in the best. No doubt, it is ridiculous enough to see people commanding absurd things to be done, only to manifest their power; but this is certain, the capricious tyrant is better obeyed, than the man of gentleness and forbearance, who refines too much on the dictates of his own compassion and suffers himself to be persuaded out of his will, because it seems troublesome to his servant to comply with it. Check, therefore, the first appearance of demur, or expostulation in one you desire to retain, to prevent subsequent animosities; and turn away him forthwith, who is guilty of the same trespass, without the pretence of merit to give a colour to his audacity.

Trusting them with secrets.] Few friends are to be trusted with secrets. Servants never, if it is possible to be avoided. Once at their mercy, they grow insolent and make no difficulty to withhold their service, when they know you dare not exact it.   What a lamentable figure must that family make where subordination is reversed and the master, instead of commanding, is forced to obey.

You are further to observe, that servants are commonly a barren soil in point of gratitude and, however lavishly you scatter your favours, seldom think themselves obliged to make any return.   Like wild beasts, you may bribe them for a while, into something like a relenting softness ; but, upon the first distate, they return to their natural fierceness, and forget they ever had any reason to be thankful.   They ever interpret your favours as their due, and, though they loudly repine when they are withheld, never make acknowledgments when they are bestowed. In that conceit, the more liberality appears on your side, the more sufficiency breaks out on theirs; and, immediately on being ruffled, they bid you provide yourself.

Rather than be in a servant's debt, never keep one at all; for, if by way of convenience to yourself, you should run into arrear with them, without making them an instant requital, they will take care to do it for you; and, assure yourself, it is no good husbandry to suffer them, in any thing, to be their own carvers.

Servants not to be oppressed.] Having proceeded thus far to secure you from being injured by them, I shall now drop a hint or two on the other side of the question, to dissuade you from being the aggressor. In order to this, behave to them with mildness and affability; not passionately abusing them, nor peevishly cavilling with them, to gratify your own splenetic humour; but giving orders with decency and reprehending faults with temper; that conviction may wait on the one and respect on the other. Nothing more impairs authority than a too frequent, or indiscreet exertion of it; were thunder itself to be continual, it would excite no more terror than the noise of a mill, and we should sleep in tranquillity when it roared the loudest. If ever then you give way to the transports of anger, let it be extremely rare; and, never, without the highest provocation.

But used with lenity.] If your do-
mestics fall sick in your service, remember you are their patron, as
well as their master; and let your
humanity flow freely for their preservation.   Not only remit their labours, but let them have all the assistance of food and physick, which
the malady requires.

Again; never let your ear be too
curious in listening to their conversation.   Passages will sometimes
occur among the best servants, that
will argue much levity and little respect; yet are void of rancour and,
as not expected to be over-heard,
are unfit for your notice or resentment.

In one word, rather exceed your
contract with them, than make the

least abatement. What is a trifle
to you, is of importance to them;
and nothing is more reasonable, than
to let them be gainers, in proportion to the time they have spent in
your service. As I would advise
you to keep them close to their business; so I recommend it to you,
likewise, to indulge them, now and
then, in certain hours of recreation.
Their lives, as well as ours, ought
to have their intervals of sunshine;
it keeps them in temper, health and
spirits and is really their due, in
equity, though you may, politically,
bestow it as an act of grace. To conclude on this head, if they have any
peculiar whims in their devotions,
leave their consciences free; you
may take what care you please of
their moral conduct; but in their
opinions, they are accountable to
none but God and themselves.

Taking apprentices.] **If you take an apprentice, do not let the bribe of so much money paid down at signing his indentures, or the prospect of a seven-years service induce you to accept one of an untoward disposition, evil inclinations, or unprincipled in virtue and good manners. It is not to be imagined what disorder such will create in your family and what vexation to yourself. For the sake of good qualities, sober education and a tractable, obliging temper, abate in the consideration. Peace is worth infinitely more than money, since money cannot purchase it; and, if such a one should fall to your lot, treat him more like a son than a servant. Remember that he is descended from your equal and that he will, one day, be the same himself. Nor,** when that day comes, have occasion to blush at reproaches he may justly make, and you will be unable to answer. In fine, look back into your own life, to recollect what you suffered, or expected, when in the same circumstances yourself; and looking forward, imagine what sort of treatment you should wish a master should use to a child of your own.

Choice of a wife.] I have before promised you to treat more at large of your choice of a wife. This is now a proper place to make it good; for, though the topic is, at present, much too early for your consideration, I am willing thus far to disarm death of his sting; and, while I yet live, give you the instructions, which, when more seasonable, may be out of my power.

Marriage.] And first, with regard
to marriage itself. As a duty to
nature and the commonwealth, I
cannot help recommending it ; but,
with regard to your own easy passage through life, I am half inclined
to the contrary. The shrewd Mr.
Osborne, in his Advice to his Son, is
pleased to insinuate, that it is the
creature of policy only ;   adding,
" the wily priests (Roman Catholic)
" are so tender of their own conve-
" niencies, as to forbid all marriage
" to themselves, upon a heavy pu-
" nishment, as they do polygamy
" unto others.   Now, if nothing
" capable of the name of felicity,
" was ever, by men or angels, found
" to be denied to the priesthood,
" may not marriage be strongly sus-
" pected to be by them thought out
" of the list, though, to render it

" more glib to the wider swallow of
" the long-abused laity, they have
" gilt it with the glorious epithet of
" sacrament!" I will add no com-
ment on this passage, but leave you
to make what conclusion you please.

However, if you rather incline to
venture on this critical state, I charge
you to look upon it as a point, on
which your whole happiness and
prosperity depend and make your
choice with a becoming gravity and
concern. I charge you, likewise,
with equal earnestness, if, by ill fortune, or ill conduct, your affairs
should be in ruins, not to make marriage an expedient to repair them.
I do not know a worse kind of hypocrisy, than to draw in the innocent and unsuspecting by false ap-
pearances, to make but one step

from ease and affluence, to all the disappointment, shame, and misery of a broken fortune. If, therefore, you must sink, sink alone, nor load yourself with the intolerable reflection that you have undone a woman who trusted you, and entailed misery on your offspring, who may have reason to look on you with abhorrence for having cursed them with being.

Till, therefore, you are not only in a thriving way yourself, but have a fair prospect that wedlock will, at least, be no incumbrance to your fortunes, never suffer yourself to think of it. The portions, received with wives, pay so large an interest by the increase of family expences, that, in the end, the husband can hardly be said to be a gainer. Do not be deceived, therefore, with that bait; but build on your own bottom; and caculate your charge, as if there was no such thing as a fortune to be depended upon at all.

Which done, proceed in your choice, on the following rational principles.

Let her be of a family not vain of their name, title, nor antiquity; those additions on her side, being certain matter of insult to the defects of yours; but remarkable for their simplicity of manners and integrity of life. Let her own character be clear and spotless, and all her pride be founded on her innocence. The blemishes of parents, however, unjustly, are a reproach to the children; nor can time wear it

out, nor merit itself efface the re-
membrance.

Let her also be alike free from
deformity and hereditary diseases.
The one being always and the other
often entailed on the breed, and
witnessing the father's indiscretion
from generation to generation.

Beauty.] Neither fix your eye on
a celebrated beauty ! It is a property
hard to possess and harder to secure.
To such an one a husband is but an
appendix. She will not only rule,
but tyrannise ; and the least demur
to the most capricious of her humours, will be attended with the
keenest upbraidings and invectives ;
the most cordial repentance that she
threw herself away on one, so insensible of the honour he had received,

and the most sincere resolutions to make herself amends by the first opportunity.

Notwithstanding these reasons, do not wholly despise harmony of shape, or elegance of features. Women are called the fair sex and, therefore, some degree of beauty is supposed almost indispensable. No doubt, it is the first object of desire and what greatly contributes to continue it fresh and undecaying. It is, likewise, often seen to be derived from the mother to the child and, therefore, as an accomplishment universally admired and coveted, to be esteemed worthy the caresses of the wise, as well as the pursuit of the libertine for a prey.

Good-nature.] What we call good-nature, is another ingredient of such importance in a matrimonial state, that, without it, the concord can never be compleat, nor the enjoyment sincere. On this account, it is both allowable and even expedient to make some experiments beforehand on the temper that is to blend, or ferment for life with your own. If you find it fickle and wavering, she will sometimes storm like March, and sometimes weep like April; not only with cause, but for want of it. If sluggish and insensible, her whole life will be a dead calm of insipidity, without joy for your prosperity, concern for your misfortunes, or spirit to assist in preventing the one, or forwarding the other. If testy and quarrelsome, you will cherish a hornet in your bosom and feel its sting every other moment in your heart.

Or, if morose and sullen, your dwelling will be melancholy as a charnel-house; and you will be impatient for a funeral, though almost indifferent whether hers, or your own. But you must not be too scrupulously exact in this scrutiny; there are none of these jewels without flaws and the very best method of enduring their faults is to remove your own.

A good manager.] This, however, bear always in mind, that if she is not frugal, if she is not what is called a good manager; if she does not pique herself on her knowledge of family affairs and laying out money to the best advantage, let her be ever so sweetly tempered, gracefully made, or elegantly accomplished, she is no wife for a tradesman; and all those, otherwise, amiable ta-

Ients, will but open just as many ways to ruin. I remember, on the wedding night of an acquaintance, where I was a guest, a motion was made, to pass an hour at an old game called *Pictures* and *Mottos*. The manner of it is, for every person in turn, as he is called upon, to furnish out a device for the painter, with a short sentence by way of explanation. The bride began it, by addressing herself first to her husband, who readily gave for his conceit, *a yoke of oxen* and for his motto, *let us draw equally*. This is the only true condition of matrimony; and nothing is more reasonable than that, as one has the whole burthen of getting money, the other should make economy her principal study, in order to preserve it. In short, remember your mother, who was so exquisitely versed in this art, that her dress, her table, and every other particular appeared rather splendid than otherwise, and yet good housewifery was the foundation of all ; and her bills, to my certain knowledge, were a fourth less than most of her neighbours, who had hardly cleanliness, or decency to boast, in return for their aukward prodigality.

Religious disposition.] It would not be amiss neither, if she you chuse, had rather a religious turn, than otherwise. Her conduct will be the more exemplary, her life more rigidly exact, her authority more punctually revered. She will be less at leisure to follow and less disposed to admire the vanities that bewitch the rest of her sex ; but if her piety should degenerate into superstition,

or enthusiasm, she is, from that moment, a lost creature. Either the
domineering spirit of holy pride, will
turn your house into an inquisition,
or the absurd terrors of a hurt imagination, make it resemble the cell of
a penitent convict.

Portion.] In the affair of portion as,
on the one hand, your conduct ought
to be provident and wary, so, on the
other, it ought to be genteel and
noble. Nothing can be more sordid
than to bargain for a wife, as you
would for a horse, and advance or
demur in your suit, as interest rose
or fell ; and, if she you solicit, should
betray too strong an attachment to
the like mercenary motives, be assured, she is too selfish to make either
a fast friend, a decent wife, or a tender parent. Fly from such, there-

fore, the moment the Smithfield genius breaks out! but do not fly to
one who has nothing but beauty, or,
if you please, affection to recommend
her! A fair wife with empty pock-
ets is like a noble house without furniture, showy, but useless; as an
odious one with abundance, resem-
bles fat lands in the fens, rich, but
uninhabitable. Let an agreeable
person then first invite your affections, good qualities fix them and
mutual interest tie the indissoluble
knot.

Of the two, as reasonable happiness is the end of life, if your circumstances will bear it, rather please
your fancy in one you like, than sacrifice your domestic peace, to the
possession of wealth, you will never
be able to enjoy. But, if the nar-

rowness of your fortune will not allow you such an indulgence, tremble
to think of the unavoidable consequences! For, if happiness does not
consist in abundance, be assured it
flies from necessity! and though the
protestations of unextinguishable
passion make a very good figure in
poetry, they have very little relation
to common sense. Besides, though
many have flattered themselves that,
by taking a wife out of the arms of
affliction, the condescension, the
obligation, would warrant a suitable
return of gratitude and affection, I
have known such as have been mi-
serably disappointed. Few minds
are strong enough to bear prosperity;
is it a wonder, therefore, that it
should turn a weak woman's brain
and that she should make her demands in point of figure, prodigality

and expence, not according to her own birth, fortune, or expectations, but yours?

Poor relations.] However, if all this is not sufficient to deter you from such a choice, at least, take care, that she is not surrounded with hungry relations; for, if she is, they will throng about you like horse-leaches; and, by the connivance, artifice, or importunity of your wife, either beg, borrow, or steal your substance, till they have pluck'd you as bare as the jay in the fable.

At all events take this along with you; there is not a perfection either of body, or mind, to be met with in low life, which is not to be as easily attained in high; and this is certain, that a great fortune gives no adamantine quality to the heart; and, if opportunity favours, she, who has that advantage and almost every other, may be won by address and assiduity in as little time, as she who is void of all.

In my first sketch of this essay, I expatiated, I fear a little too largely, on the means of rendering your courtship pleasing to the person you desire to win. In this, therefore, I shall endeavour to be as brief as possible. Indeed, in these cases, Nature is the best tutor, and the eloquence of unfeigned passion more persuasive than the most artful strokes of the most accomplished orators.

Courtship.] There is not, however, any thing more necessary, than so to regulate the progress of this insinu-

H

ating impulse, as to have it thoroughly at your command; for, if you give it too large scope, instead of being master of it, it will be the master of you; and you will thenceforward lay your weakness so open and appear so manifestly in the power of your mistress, that the pleasure of tyrannizing will be irresistible and she will exert her sovereignty to the utmost, only to gratify her own pride with the barbarous experiment.

Nor is this the only necessary caution you are to observe. As you are to keep as much as possible out of her power, so, on the contrary, you are to endeavour as much as possible, to ensnare her into yours. To which end, it will be expedient, to make your visits always contri-

bute to her pleasure. Never be
seen but in your gayest mood; be
prepared with the most entertaining
topics of conversation; be furnished
with some slight, but welcome present; never stay till the spirit of the
dialogue is exhausted, nay, sometimes take your leave, when she
seems most desirous you should stay;
nor ever mention love, till you are,
in a manner, certain, she is half ripe
to make it the first petition in her
prayers; and, even then, let it be so
mixed with raillery, that in case you
have deceived yourself in your con-
clusions, you may, without a blush,
laugh off your own disappointment
and her triumph together. If she
indicates that you treat so serious
an affair too lightly and appears
only displeased that you are no deeper enamoured, the transition is very

H 2

easy to a more passionate deportment and you may carry your point
by arguments, assiduites and services, tho' joke and humour failed.

Wedding day.] Do not distinguish
your wedding day too ostentatiously, or suffer it to pass away without
proper marks of acknowledgment.
Let it wear a sober smile, such as
would become your bride and you
for life, nor be convulsed with riot-
ous laughter, that leaves tears in the
eyes and heaviness at the heart as
soon as the fit is over.

Complaisance after marriage.] Suffer me, likewise, to remind you that,
though most men marry, few live
happily; which manifestly proves,
that there is more art necessary to
keep the affection alive, than to pro-

cure its gratification. But, as this is a point of the highest importance, let me advise you to study it, as the science of life. In order to which, do not permit yourself to think cheaply of your wife, or neglect her because you are secure in possession. It is impossible, that a woman should not be grievously shocked to see the servile lover transformed, at once, into the tyrant husband. Assure yourself there are but very few steps between indifference, neglect, contempt and aversion. Therefore, if you have any respect for your own repose, let your first transports be moderate and, when over, do not so much as with a look, betray either satiety, or repentance, but let the same chearfulness appear on your brow, the same tenderness in your eyes, the same obliging turn in your behaviour and give her daily and hourly proofs, if possible, that she is as dear to you as ever. Above all things, never let her imagine it a penance to you to stay at home, or that you prefer any company whatever to hers. On the contrary, let her share with you in all your pleasures, and find frequent opportunities to induce her to think it will be her own fault, if she is not the happiest woman in the world. By these means, she will not only dread to lose your favour, but, from inclination and gratitude, endeavour to preserve it. Those husbands are fools who think to terrify their wives into subjection; for whatever is yielded through compulsion, will be resumed, as soon as ever occasion offers; and those that restrain the unwilling, experience as much trouble to keep them in obedience, as pleasure in being obeyed.

Should ever this delightful calm be ruffled by any little escape of peevishness, or anger, do not widen the breach with bitter expressions, or give way to a dogged sullenness, that may prolong resentment till it becomes unappeasable. Where frailty is mutual, offences will be the same, and so should forbearance and forgiveness too. Love, like charity, should cover a multitude of sins and there is no room for malice in the heart which harbours that amiable guest. Interpret favourably then every incident that provokes your disgust; if obliged to complain, do it gently and dispassionately and gladly receive the first acknowledgment as a very sufficient atonement.

Nor vainly and obstinately insist on her submitting first. Depend upon it, the most obstinate of the two is the most foolish; and it will be for your credit that the odds of wisdom should be on your side. To say the truth, no woman would marry, if she expected to be a slave and there can be no freedom where there is no will. In all trifling matters then, leave her to her own discretion; it will be of advantage to you on more important occasions; and she will chearfully forbear interfering in your province, if she finds herself undisturbed in her own.

As to what remains, have but one table, one purse, and one bed. Either separate will be attended with separate interests; and there cannot be too many ties to strengthen an union, which, though calculated to last for life, is of such a cobweb kind, as often to wear out before the ho-ney-moon.

I conclude on these domestic articles, with advising you, to be modest in the furniture of your house and not over curious in your bills of fare. Let there be always such plenty, that, if any accidental guest dropt in, you need not blush, or apologize for his entertainment; but no superfluity at your own board, or waste at your servants. Even when you entertain, which I hope will be as seldom as possible, do not swell out the pride of a day to such an exorbitant size, as to make a reduction of your expences necessary for a month to come. Remember your whole life ought to be of a piece and

that, though you were to entertain
a lord, a tradesman must defray the
charge. Neither think it beneath
you to be your own caterer; it will
save you many a pound at the year's
end and your kitchen will be much
better supplied into the bargain.

A maxim of the same prudent nature, is to go to market always with
ready money; for whoever runs in
debt for provisions, had better borrow at ten per cent. and will find it
easier to balance his accounts.

To which may be added, that such
idle profusion only excites envy in
your inferiors, hatred in your equals
and indignation in your superiors,
who are, moreover, apt to think,
every extraordinary item in your
banquet is made an article in their

bill; and, therefore, will incline,
with a certain witty duke, to deal
with one who scarce affords himself
necessaries, and dine with you.

Education of children.] As to what
concerns the education of your children, recollect your own.   Recollect the precepts I here present you
with for the conduct of your future
life and you cannot be at a loss to
render them wise, honest, and thriving men.   First take care of their
health, then their morals, and finally
of their making their way success-
fully through the world.   Under the
last head, I recommend it to you,
in the most earnest manner, not
only to make them scholars, or
even gentlemen, in case your fortune
will afford the means, but men of
business too.   It is the surest way

to preserve an estate when got, to
amass together money enough to
purchase one, or keep the wolf of
poverty from the door, in case of
misfortunes.   How many descend-
ants of eminent citizens have I seen,
undone, by a neglect of this rule;
who set up early in polite life, have
been even ashamed of their origin
and would, if possible, have disown-
ed their fathers, to whose indulgence
and application they owed the very
means of living idly and prodigally;
the only title they had to be ranked
among the gentry !

I shall close all, with two important hints, which as more fitted for
the consideration of your riper years,
I have purposely reserved for the last.

Politics.] In England, it is impos-

sible for a man who has a vote to
give, not to have some concern in
public affairs. The talk of the times,
the very news of the day will make
him a party whether he will, or not.
In your own defence then and even
to preserve yourself from the fallacies
of interested men, make yourself acquainted with the history of the British constitution in general, and that
of your own times in particular; the
right of the subject, the privilege of
parliament, the power of the crown,
the pretences of patriots, and the designs of ministers; the rise, growth,
extent and importance of our commerce; the expediency of taxes, the
danger of a military force, and the
real views of all the different parties
that have worked the nation into its
present ferment: but make this your
amusement, not your business, that

when you are called upon to name your representative in parliament, you may be able to judge for yourself of the virtue or ability of the candidate; explain the services you expect from him and, if need be, furnish out a test to know how far he may be depended upon, to enforce privileges, redress grievances, and stand in the gap between the encroachments of power, however disguised and the liberties and properties of a defenceless people. But I charge you upon my blessing to wear the badge of no party whatever. Be assured it is a badge of slavery and, under the pretence of procuring you esteem and confidence will render you unworthy of both. To be free is to be independent and, if you would continue so, consult your own conscience, and act only according to its dictates. Despise flattery on one side, disdain corruption on the other, and let the venal of all ranks know, that your traffic is not in infamy, nor your gains the wages of corruption.

Religion.] Religion, with which I conclude, I would have you both awfully reverence and devoutly practice; not as the hypocrites do, as a sort of commutation with the world, for living like a cannibal and preying upon your fellow-creatures. God is a spirit; worship him in spirit and in truth; not with unmeaning jargon and ostentatious ceremonies. Come before him with the incense of an innocent and virtuous life and, wherever you address him, either with prayer, or praise, he will not be slow to hear, nor backward to accept the grateful offering. As to believe you are always within the reach and under the care of his Providence, is an everlasting source of comfort, so to remember you are ever in his eye and that all your actions, words and thoughts are registered before him, will preserve you sinless, though surrounded with temptations.

Finally, whilst I would have you consider the present life as a state of probation and the future, as the certain rectifier and rewarder of all the good and evil committed here; yet I say live innocently, live honestly, live usefully if possible, apart from that interesting consideration. Men discharge their duty to the world, who act uprightly, whatever is their motive; but they are best acquitted to themselves, who love and practice virtue, for its own divine perfections.

THE END.

T. Gillet, Printer, Wild-Court.

The following works are edited by John Joseph Stockdale.

1.—Second Edition, in one large volume, 8vo. Illustrated with Eleven elegantly drawn Plates, containing 108 Subjects, and a map of the world, price only 10s. 6d. or elegantly calf gilt, 13s.

Encyclopædia for Youth;

OR AN

ABRIDGMENT OF ALL THE SCIENCES,

For the use of Schools of both Sexes.

2.—Elegantly printed in Royal Octavo, on the finest Paper, and hot-pressed, Price One Guinea; in Demy Octavo 10s. 6d. or in 12mo. 6s. 6d. embellished with a capital Portrait of the Northern Hero, from the celebrated Painting in the Possession of Louis XIV. Dedicated to the Hero of the East, the Marquis WELLESLEY,

THE HISTORY OF CHARLES XII.

KING OF SWEDEN.

BY M. DE VOLTAIRE.

To which are prefixed,

ANECDOTES

OF THE CZAR PETER THE GREAT OF RUSSIA,

AN ESSAY ON HISTORY, &c.

Translated from the last French edition.

French Editions uniform with the above translation, will be ready in a few days.

It is necessary to observe, that *this translation*, made from the most celebrated French edition, bears scarcely any resemblance to those heretofore published in England.

As the Military operations on the Continent are become of such general interest, and are carried so far northward, the Publisher begs leave to recommend the above History, which gives more insight into the mutual advantages and difficulties of the contending armies than perhaps any other work extant.

CPSIA information can be obtained at www.ICGtesting.com
Printed in the USA
BVOW09s1007070415

395057BV00016B/127/P